The Unrepeatable IF...

The Unrepeatable IF...

Steve Bell

A Methuen Paperback

For Heather, William, Joe and Patrick

This collection first published in Great Britain in 1986
by Methuen London Ltd
11 New Fetter Lane, London EC4P 4EE

The strips first published by *The Guardian* 1985 and 1986

Designed by Brian Homer
Edited by Steve Bell and Brian Homer

Typeset by P & W Typesetters
202 Hagley Road, Edgbaston, Birmingham

Made and printed in Great Britain

British Library Cataloguing in Publication Data
Bell, Steve
  The unrepeatable "If..."
  I. Title   II. The guardian
  741,5'942   PN6738

ISBN 0 413 14440 2

Hi! I'M A DOG! I'M **STREET SMART** AND I LIKE A **WALK**, BUT TAKE A WALK DOWN ANY STREET TODAY AND WHAT DO YOU SEE? **ADVERTS**. ADVERTS EVERYWHERE YOU LOOK. **WHAT ARE THEY ADVERT--ISING**? **I'LL TELL YOU**: ON THE AVERAGE WALK I LIKE TO **RECITE** WHAT'S **ON OFFER** AS I PASS. GENERALLY, THIS IS HOW IT GOES:

"**BOOZE; FAGS; FAGS; BOOZE; BOOZE; CARS; FAGS; BOOZE**..."

OF COURSE, YOU GET THE OCCASIONAL BIT OF **VARIETY**: "**BOOZE; FAGS; FROZEN GOURMET DINNERS; FAGS**..." AND THEN, IF THERE'S AN **ELECTION** IN THE OFFING YOU HAVE THE ADDED BONUS: "**BOOZE; FAGS; TORIES; BOOZE; BOOZE....**"!!

ADVERTS? PISS ON 'EM!!

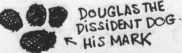 DOUGLAS THE DISSIDENT DOG — HIS MARK

5

THE DEVASTATING CLIMAX OF THE NEVER ENDING SOAP SAGA THAT WRENCHED A NATION'S TEAR DUCTS:

MAGGIE GO HOME

SEEKING TO TERMINATE HERSELF WITH EXTREME PREJUDICE BY LEAPING INTO THE CHASM OF DOOM, MARGARET HAS DISCOVERED IT TO BE CLOSED:

— © Steve Bell 1985 ~

...SO THERE YOU HAVE IT, DUCKS, — NO MORE CHASM OF DOOM!! THAT'S LIFE, EH? WERE YOU TRYING TO BUMP YOURSELF OFF?? PERHAPS I COULD BE OF SOME ASSISTANCE?? HALF A MO....

GOBLIN & TROLL

1044

'ERE WE ARE — A COUPLE OF SWIFT TAPS FROM THIS AND YOUR TROUBLES WILL BE A THING OF THE PAST!!

THANKS AWFULLY, BUT I REALLY WOULDN'T WANT YOU TO PUT YOURSELF OUT ON MY ACCOUNT!

DON'T WORRY — IT'LL BE A PLEASURE!

KLANNG!

KLANNG!

YOU SEE — IT'S NO USE — I'M INDESTRUCTIBLE — YOU'LL ONLY DENT YOUR BALL!!

DENTED BALLS? WHO'S GOT DENTED BALLS?

BE QUIET, YOU VULGAR LITTLE GOBLIN!!

VULGAR LITTLE GOBLINS WITH DENTED BALLS!? WHAT'S BEEN GOING ON BEHIND MY BACK, MARGARET??

© Steve Bell 1985

DENIS? IS THAT YOU?? WHERE AM I?

1045

YOU'VE BEEN OUT COLD UNDERNEATH A HEAP OF RED BOXES, MARGARET, BUT I WANT TO KNOW WHAT THIS GOBLIN'S BALLS BUSINESS IS ALL ABOUT!!!

GOOD LORD! IT'S ALL BEEN A FRIGHTFUL DREAM!

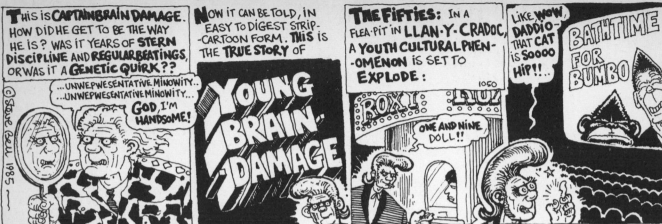

YOUNG BRAIN-DAMAGE

SOON, YOUNG BRAIN-DAMAGE WAS TO FACE ONE OF THE MOST TESTING AND TRAUMATIC MOMENTS OF HIS ENTIRE LIFE:

HEY, DOZO MAN, LIKE WE DID SOME NEAT RIPPING THERE! C'MON BACK TO MY PAD, DAD AND WE'LL HAVE A FRIED EGG AND A CUP O' * CAMP!!

ROXY

* FIFTIES CULT FOOD

BUT:

HEY, MAN— LIKE IT'S A LETTER!

OH NOOO MAN! IT'S THE **@☆ *@ING CALLUP! LIKE, I GOTTA JOIN THE **@ING ARMY!!!

AND SO, YOUNG BRAIN-DAMAGE IS INSTANTLY POLITICISED:

SOUTH WALES TORY TEDS OPPOSE MILITARISM

SOUTH WALES TORY TEDS SAY: CUT THE CALL UP!!

YOUNG BRAIN-DAMAGE

BY AN INCREDIBLE STROKE OF LUCK, YOUNG BRAIN-DAMAGE IS SELECTED AS CONSERVATIVE CANDIDATE FOR THE LLAN-Y-CRADOC CONSTITUENCY, AND GETS OUT OF THE ARMY

I NOMINATE PRIVATE BRAIN-DAMAGE!

I SECOND THAT!!

LLAN-Y-CRADOC CONSERVATIVE ASSOCIATION.

CARRIED UNANIMOUSLY!

THERE FOLLOWS A VIGOROUS CAMPAIGN

THE COUNTRY NEEDS BRAIN-DAMAGE

YEW BACCER OFF BOYO!

PUT BRAIN-DAMAGE FIRST CONSERVATIVE

YOU'VE NEVER HAD IT SO GOOD!

AND THE TENSE MOMENT OF THE FINAL COUNT:

AS RETURNING OFFICER FOR THE LLAN-Y-CRADOC CONSTITUENCY, I DECLARE THAT THE NUMBER OF VOTES CAST WAS AS FOLLOWS: BASTARD, HUW [LABOUR]: THIRTY EIGHT THOUSAND NINE HUNDRED AND FIFTY THREE VOTES; BRAIN-DAMAGE, MICHAEL TARZAN WINSTON POPEYE [CONSERVATIVE]: NIL.

11

YOUNG BRAIN-DAMAGE

THE EXPERIENCE OF NATIONAL SERVICE, WAS TO HAVE A VERY **TRAUMATIC** EFFECT ON THE YOUNG BRAIN-DAMAGE....

1054

NYAAADAHURP! HIP YARP!!

LIKE, HEY MAN - THIS CAT TALKS JIVE!!

NYAHURNA HORNA HOONA HURNA HIP HUP HUURP!!

I 'HEAR YOU TALKIN', DADDIO, BUT, LIKE, WHAT ARE YOU SAYIN' TO ME? I DON'T DIG, Y'DIG??

...LIKE, WHAT'S WITH THE SHEET MAN?

HURR HIP HURRR!

OH NOOOOOO MAN! NOT MY REAGAN QUIFF, MAN! NOOOO!!

©steve Bell 1985

YOUNG BRAIN-DAMAGE

FACED WITH THE LOSS OF HIS QUIFF AND THE POSSIBLE LOSS OF MORE THAN THAT, YOUNG BRAIN-DAMAGE INVENTS A CUNNING PLAN:

OH MAAAN!! LIKE, MY QUIFF IS GONE FOREVER!

OKAY CHAPS - YOU HAVE ALL BEEN SELECTED TO TAKE PART IN SOME RATHER SPECIAL TESTS FOR THESE NEW ISSUE RADIATION-PROOF ARMY SHORTS!

1055

IT'S FAIRLY STRAIGHTFORWARD - ALL YOU CHAPS HAVE TO DO IS STAND HERE AT POINT Ⓐ IN THE SHORTS, WHILE WE DETONATE A THERMO-NUCLEAR DEVICE HERE AT POINT Ⓑ. ANY QUESTIONS?

LIKE *@⊕* THAT FOR A GAME OF SOLDIERS, MAN - THAT IS STRICTLY FOR THE BIRDS!!

©steve Bell '85

ER...EXCUSE ME, SIR, MAN...LIKE I GOT THIS SUDDEN URGENT AMBITION TO BECOME SECRETARY OF STATE FOR DEFENCE, BUT, LIKE, I NEED LEAVE TO BECOME A TORY M.P. FIRST MAN, SIR

JOLLY GOOD! THAT SHOWS INITIATIVE, BRAIN-DAMAGE!

ON BOARD THE **U.S.S. RIBBITZ,**

OKAY — AS MEMBERS OF THE **ELITE TOADFORCE,** YOU HAVE TO KNOW SOMETHIN' ABOUT JUST WHAT IN HELL IS GOIN' ON IN BEIRUT....

RIBBIT

RIBBIT

FIRST OFF YOU GOT THE **PALESTINIANS,** THEN YOU GOT THE **SHI'ITES,** THEN YOU GOT THE **CHRISTIANS.....**

1059

...THEN YOU GOT THE **DRUZE** THEN YOU GOT THE **AMAL** THEN YOU GOT THE **LEBANESE ARMY,** THEN YOU GOT THE **UNITED NATIONS.** YOU GOTTA TRY AND KEEP ALL THIS STUFF CLEAR IN YOUR MIND....

...BEFORE YOU **GO IN** AND KILL'EM ALL!!

© Steve Bell 1985

REMEMBER — A TOAD AIN'T JUST AN **AMPHIBIAN** ...

NOSUH RIBBIT!

RIBBIT

...**A TOAD** IS A **CAREFULLY DESIGNED, FINELY TUNED KILLING MACHINE** ...

1060

YASSUH RIBBIT!!

...**A TOAD** HAS GOTTA BE ABLE TO **KILL** ANYTIME ANYWHERE, ANYWAY POSSIBLE ...

RIBBIT

© Steve Bell '85

...I'M NOT JUST TALKIN' ABOUT CIVIL WAR, SEA WAR, AIR WAR, OR LIMITED **NOOCULAR WAR,** I'M TALKIN' ABOUT **TOADAL WAR!**

RIBBIT

14

ON BOARD THE **U.S.S. RIBBITZ:**

OKAY TOADFORCE - PIN BACK YOUR **AURAL CAVITIES** - NOW I'M TALKIN' **TOAD TACTICS!**

..THIS IS **AN OLD PROBLEM** - TO GET THE **TOAD** OUT OF THE **POND** OVER THE **ROAD** AND INTO THE **HOLE**. THIS IS COMPLICATED BY THE FACT THAT WE **DON'T KNOW** WHERE THE **HOLE** IS......

PLUS, AS YOU GUYS WELL KNOW, A **TOAD** IN THE **ROAD** IS AS GOOD AS **NO TOAD AT ALL.** THIS PROBLEM IS KNOWN TECHNICALLY AS **NEGOTIATING** A **NO TOAD ZONE** WITHOUT **TOADTALITIES** ....

BASICALLY, THERE ARE **TWO WAYS** TO DO IT. EITHER WE EMPLOY A **SURROGATE TOAD** TO COME FROM **BEHIND,** OR WE TAKE OUT THE **ENTIRE HEMISPHERE!**

FINALLY, TOADS, WHEN THE **SHIT'S HIT THE FAN** AND **BURST RIGHT IN YOUR FACE** ....

...I MEAN **THAT MOMENT** WHEN **TALL, TOUGH-TALKIN' TOADS** HAVE BEEN MADE TO **LOOK SMALL** ...

...**THAT** IS THE **MOMENT** FOR **TOAD VENGEANCE!!** IT DON'T MATTER THAT WE **DON'T KNOW** WHO EXACTLY TO WREAK **VENGEANCE** ON..

ALL THAT MATTERS IS THAT THE **WORLD GETS THE MESSAGE:** "**NOBODY, BUT NOBODY GOADS A TOAD!**"

LOOSELY INSPIRED BY BILL GRIFFITH + GILBERT SHELTON

15

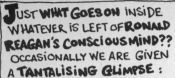

JUST WHAT GOES ON INSIDE WHATEVER IS LEFT OF RONALD REAGAN'S CONSCIOUS MIND?? OCCASIONALLY WE ARE GIVEN A TANTALISING GLIMPSE:

WHERE SHALL I STICK HIM, BUD?

AW, JUST LEAN HIM AGAINST THE WALL AWHILE...

1063.

AWWW RATS! - THE WIRING'S ALL WRONG!! HOW CAN I INSTALL THE PRESIDENT IF THE GODDAMN WIRING'S ALL WRONG!!

NNNNN HEY... BUB!.. NNNN..

HOLY SHIT!! HE SPOKE - AND HE AIN'T EVEN PLUGGED IN YET!!

...NNN BOY, I SAW 'DUMBO' LAST NIGHT!

© Steve Bell 1985.

RON IS SPEAKING WITHOUT MECHANICAL AIDS....

YEAH!.. I SAW 'DUMBO' LAST NIGHT - SUCH AN INSPIRING MOVIE!!

I DON'T BELIEVE IT!

...NOW I KNOW WHAT TO DO NEXT TIME THERE'S A HOSTAGE CRISIS....

WHAT THE HELL'S HE TALKIN' ABOUT?

...I JUST GOTTA HIRE A BIG SQUAD OF ELEPHANTS, GET 'EM TO GROW THEIR EARS REAL BIG - WE HAVE THE TECHNOLOGY...

1064

....DOSE 'EM UP WITH CASCARA AND SPECIAL 'K', THEN SEND 'EM FLYIN' OVER THE LEBANON!!

© Steve Bell 1985 ~

British Justice

"It's the Best Justice money can buy!"
says **79** year old sexual athlete **QUINT**
('e's not skint!) LORD HIGH CHANCELLOR OF ENGLAND
VORSPRUNG DURCH BANG 'EM UP JOHN!

DURING THE COURSE OF MY INVESTIGATIONS INTO ADVERTISING I'VE COME TO DISTINGUISH THE **BASIC TYPES** AND **METHODS** THAT ADVERTS USE. THE ONE I **HATE MOST** is THE **PRESTIGE APPEAL** TO **STRAIGHT XENOPHOBIA** — YOU KNOW WHAT I MEAN: 'OUR JUDGES DRESS UP IN **FUNERAL DRAG** AND SIT AROUND ON **DEAD SHEEP** — HOW INSPIRINGLY **TRADITIONAL** — THEY MUST BE THE **BEST** IN THE WORLD' — FUCK 'EM, I SAY!!!

19

THE VENGEANCE OF BUMBO

HEY!.. IF YOU FLY, AND YOU'RE BIG AND FULL OF ENOUGH SHIT, YOU CAN TERRORISE THE ENTIRE GLOBE!

SOON, THE INCONTINENT FLYING ELEPHANT MADE AN IMPORT- ANT DISCOVERY:

1067

UNTIL:

OKAY!! FLY ME TO DISNEYLAND OR I'LL BLOW A HOLE IN YOUR HAIRSTYLE!

HOLY *@☆!! HOW DID YOU GET THERE?

I LIVED IN THAT TREE YOU JUST DESTROYED - DON'T TRY ANY FUNNY BUSINESS- I'VE WIRED YOUR ASS WITH EXPLOSIVES!!

THE VENGEANCE OF BUMBO

THE HI-JACKED FLYING ELEPHANT IS NOW 5000 FEET ABOVE DISNEYLAND

OKAY - THERE IT IS - WHADDYA WANT ME TO DO NOW??

YOU'RE GONNA DUMP A FIFTEEN HUNDRED POUND DOODY ON THE MAGIC CASTLE!!

WHU..?!

1068.

BUT... BUT... THAT'S MY SPIRITUAL HOME!! I'LL NEVER BE ABLE TO LIVE DOWN THE SHAME OF IT!!

JUST DO IT!

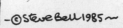

—©Steve Bell 1985~

OHHH BUMBO!

OHHH BUMBO!

OHHH BUMBO!

TO BE CONTINUED:

20

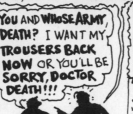

...RIBBEDABAMBOOMADA BOTTOMLINE BALLPARK BADGUYS TOADFORCE GODDAGOADER DISNEYLAND IMMEDIATEWISE

...RIBBET...HEMISPHERIC INTEREST GEOPOLITICAL PECKERPOWER GLOBAL CREDIBILITY.....HURN...

...SOVIET THREATWISE MISTER PRESIDENT DOOMSDAYBOX RIBBET MISSION IMPOSSIBLE...

1077

...DELTA TOADFORCE ACTUALLY GODDA GO INSIDE THE PRESIDENT!!

THANKS TO DAVID AUSTIN.

MEANWHILE, IN DISNEYLAND:

BUMBO - GIMME THE DOOMSDAYBOX!!

BUMBO - DO YOU HEAR ME? I'M IN CHARGE NOW - WHERE IS THE DOOMSDAY BOX???!

HEAR THIS, YA GODDAMN STOOPID ELEPHANT - WHERE IS THE DOOMSDAY BOX??

1078

OH NO! OH GAHD!! HE'S EATEN IT!! HE'S EATEN THE GODDAMN DOOMSDAY BOX!!!

HOLY GOD CHRIST, BUMBO!!! WHAT HAVE YOU DONE??!

DO YOU REALISE THAT SOVIET SUBMARINES ARE POISED TO HIT DISNEYLAND INSIDE TEN MINUTES?!!

...AND YOU HAVE GONE AND SWALLOWED THE GODDAMN DOOMSDAY BOX!! THE MAGIC KINGDOM IS NOW DEFENCELESS!!

THERE'S ONLY ONE THING WE CAN DO — WE GOTTA SEND THE DELTA TOADFORCE IN TO GET IT!!

GO FOR IT!

HUP! HUP! YOWSA!

— THANKS TO DAVID AUSTIN —

INSIDE A WELL KNOWN WORLD LEADER THE SEARCH GOES ON:

HUP! HUP! GO FOR IT!!

YOWSA!! I SEEN IT! YOU SEEN WHAT?

I SEEN THE DOOMSDAY BOX!!

DAKKA DAKKA DAKKA

THAT AIN'T THE DOOMSDAY BOX—THASSA SMALL MALIGNANT GROWTH!!

BAMMA LAMMA LAMMA

CHEESES!!! THAT WAS NO SMALL MALIGNANT GROWTH — —THAT WAS HIS BRAIN!!

— © STEVE BELL 1985 —

THANKS TO HEATHER —

26

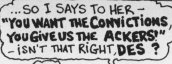
...SO I SAYS TO HER — "YOU WANT THE CONVICTIONS, YOU GIVE US THE ACKERS!" — ISN'T THAT RIGHT, DES ?

YUR.

..SO SHE SAYS TO ME : "I LIKE YOU — YOU'RE ONE OF US — YOU CAN HAVE 7·5% !!

7·5% ?? BLOOMIN' CHEEK!

...SO I SAYS TO HER: "LEAVE IT OUT !" — DO YOU KNOW WHAT THIS GEAR COST ME ?? DO YOU KNOW WHAT IT COST ??

1081

IT COST A F@*☆ OF A LOT !!

THAT'S RIGHT, DES — IT COST A F*☆@ OF A LOT ! THAT'S WHAT I TOLD HER !

SO WHAT DID SHE SAY TO THAT ?

SHE SAYS: "QUINT — I LIKE YOU — YOU'VE GOT A CHEEKY FACE — YOU CAN HAVE 16·3% UP FRONT IN YOUR HAND, NOW !"

NICE ONE!

...SO THEN I BUMP INTO THIS BLEEDIN' TEACHER, AND DO YOU KNOW WHAT THE INSOLENT LITTLE PIMPLE SAYS TO ME ?? I'LL TELL YOU WHAT SHE SAYS

SHE SAYS:"16·3% ON A BIG SALARY LIKE YOURS IS A LOT OF MONEY — ALL WE'RE BEING OFFERED IS 5% OF NOT A LOT, WHICH IS BASICALLY NOTHING AT ALL! WHAT MAKES YOU SO SPECIAL ??

CHEEKY COW !!

...SO I TELLS HER :"LISTEN, GIRLIE — I'M A JUDGE — IN ORDER TO EXERCISE MY JUDICIAL FACULTIES, I MUST BE IMMUNE FROM OUTSIDE INFLUENCES. THEREFORE SOCIETY MUST PAY ME SUFFICIENT TO KEEP MYSELF OUT OF IT."

1082.

THEN COMES THE BIT THEY CAN'T ARGUE WITH — I SAYS TO HER : "DO YOU KNOW HOW MUCH IT COSTS TO KEEP MYSELF OUT OF IT ?? HAVE YOU ANY IDEA HOW MUCH A CRATE OF CRUSTED PORT CAN SET A MAN BACK THESE DAYS ??"

A F*@☆ OF A LOT !!

THAT'S RIGHT, DES !!

1083

FUNNY OLD LIFE BEING A **JUDGE**, EH DES??

FUNNY OLD BUSINESS — UP AND DOWN UP AND DOWN!!

PORT

THE **THING I LIKE BEST** IS HAVING TO **DRESS UP** AS A CROSS BETWEEN A **BAT**, A **CROW** AND A **COCKROACH**! I LIKE THE **FISHNETS** AND THE **HIGH HEELS**!

THASS **DEAD RIGHT** QUINT

...BUT I TELL YOU — THE **BEST BIT** USED TO BE THE **OLD BLACK CAP** — THAT'S THE BIT I REALLY **MISS**!

...I'VE TRIED **DEELEY BOBBERS** BUT THEY DON'T HAVE THE **SAME IMPACT**, DO THEY DES?

NO WAY QUINT!

© Steve Bell 1985

NICE TO HAVE A **BREAK** NOW AND AGAIN, EH, DES?

THASS **DEAD RIGHT!**

© Steve Bell 1985

...COURSE, YOUR AVERAGE **SNOT-NOSED LITTLE PUNTER** DOESN'T REALISE THE **LENGTHS** WE HAVE TO **GO** TO TO GET A BIT O' **RELAXATION**

— **NO WAY** QUINT

...THERE'S THE **COST** OF A **FIRST CLASS RETURN** TO **STREATHAM** — THAT'S A **LOT** THESE DAYS

A F#@☆ OF A **LOT!**

Str'th'm

...THEN THERE'S THE **PRICE** OF A **WHEELBARROW** AT THE OTHER END....

ASTRO- F#@☆#G -NOMICAL!

SNAR!

OI!

28

Are you ever struck by the **unparalleled growth** in the number of adverts like this? Who are all these mystery conglomerates and why are they doing so nicely thank you? Who actually gives a brassfart whether the perpetrators of the latest snack weapon have described their performance with words like **Sustained Profit Growth Progress**? I'll tell you who: it's the Double Dinner Fraternity,* looking to quadruple the value of their dinner holdings.

© Steve Bell '85

15 STONE
19 STONE
23 STONE
28 STONE
35 STONE
41 STONE
50 STONE+

Nigel Lawson
and friends   getting bigger and cheekier all the time

SOMETIMES I THINK I HATE THIS SORT MOST OF ALL !!!

*   Using food lust as a metaphor for cash greed. The author (no sylph) wishes in no way to offend the fat, or those who must eat 2 dinners for medical reasons.

IT'S ALL GETTING A BIT TOO MUCH, DENIS— —WE HAVE TO GET AWAY

ANTHRAX NOW MORE POPULAR THAN THATCHER SHOCK

RHINO WRESTLING IN S. AFRICA

Club 59-83

I MEAN GET AWAY COMPLETELY- RIGHT AWAY FROM THE PRYING EYES OF THE PAPARAZZI!!

...BUT IT HAS TO BE SOMEWHERE BRITISH— —I'M ABSOLUTELY ADAMANT ABOUT THAT!!

YOU MEAN WE'RE NOT GOING TO THAT DAMNED SCHLOSS IN CUCKOO CLOCK LAND?? PRAISE THE LORD!

...WHICH IS WHY I'VE DECIDED WE'RE GOING TO ROCKALL THIS YEAR!

'KINELL!!

Steve Bell '85

IT WAS SO KIND OF OLD SQUIFFY FARTSMERE TO LEND US HIS CARAVAN

I'M NOT SO SURE ABOUT THAT, MARGARET!

...AND IT WAS SO KIND OF CAPTAIN BRAIN DAMAGE TO LOAN US A HERCULES..

I WOULDN'T BE SO SURE ABOUT THAT EITHER, MARGARET

...AND DROP US IN THE MIDDLE OF THE ATLANTIC.

© Steve Bell 1985

...AMONGST MY LOYAL SEABIRD SUBJECTS!

GORDON BENNET!!!

32

MARGARET IS ON HOLIDAY ON ROCKALL:

AHHHHH!! DENIS - SMELL THAT AIR!!

NO THANK-YOU MAG!

©Steve Bell '85

MAGNIFICENT! AND IT'S ALL BRITISH!!

1090.

I KNOW IT'S BRITISH BECAUSE IT FEELS BRITISH. THIS EARTH IS BRITISH EARTH. THESE FLOWERS ARE BRITISH FLOWERS. THOSE BIRDS ARE BRITISH BIRDS...

VAT DE FJÖERKJA TOKKENABOOT, MJÖESSES?? HEM NAARVEEJEN !!

AND I'M IRISH !

DENIS! THIS PLACE IS CRAWLING WITH FOREIGNERS!!

SURELY NOT, MARGARET?

TELEGRAPH DRINKS AGE

SOMETHING'S GOT TO BE DONE ABOUT IT — WE CAN'T ALLOW BRITISH TERRITORY.....

© Steve Bell 1985

...TO FALL INTO THE HANDS OF A BUNCH OF NORWEGIAN PADDIES!!

KNOCK KNOCK

WHAT'S THAT??

INDEED

GOOD AFTERNOON, MADAM — I'M FROM THE SOCIALIST SEABIRDS REPUBLIC OF ROCKALL IMMIGRATION CONTROL, AND I HAVE TO ASK YOU A FEW QUESTIONS:....
ARE YOU OR HAVE YOU EVER BEEN RELATED TO ANY MEMBER OF THE CONSERVATIVE PARTY?
DO YOU INTEND TO OVERTHROW BY FORCE THE GOVERNMENT OF THE S.S.R.R??
DO YOU KNOW ANY GANNETS??

WHAT DO YOU MEAN: "DO I KNOW ANY GANNETS"??

JUST FOR OUR STATISTICS MADAM... AND FINALLY I MUST POINT OUT THE CURRENCY RESTRICTIONS ON PERSONS ENTERING THE SOCIALIST SEABIRDS' REPUBLIC OF ROCKALL...

1092

YOU ARE REQUIRED BY LAW TO SURRENDER ALL CURRENCY OF ANY KIND TO A NOMINATED OFFICIAL WHO WILL EXCHANGE IT FOR TURDS. THE CURRENT RATE OF EXCHANGE IS £2·50 to 1 TURD, O.K.??

NO, THAT MOST CERTAINLY IS NOT O.K!!

© Steve Bell 1985

SO YOU WON'T COMPLY? O.K. GLORIA-FRISK HER!!

THERE'S SOMETHING CLANKING HERE!!

STOP IT! STOP IT!! THERE'S £15000 IN GOLD MARGARETS HIDDEN IN THIS THUNDERBOX!

FRISK

FRISK

THANK YOU MADAM - THAT'LL BE 6000 TURDS - IF YOU JUST SIGN HERE

WHAT ARE WE GOING TO DO NOW, DENIS? OUR CARAVAN IS CHOC FULL OF....

BUGGER IT - I'M GOING SURFING!

1093

GOOD LORD - LOOK AT THOSE BIRDS OVER THERE!

EEEYAA!

GULP GULP

...AND WHAT SORT OF BIRDS ARE YOU??

WE'RE GANNETS, MA'AM.

YOU SEEM LIKE THRUSTING, GO-AHEAD SORT OF BIRDS

YES, WE'RE THOROUGHLY GREEDY BASTARDS, MA'AM!!

HOW WOULD YOU LIKE TAX INCENTIVES TO ENABLE YOU TO CONSUME EVEN MORE?

? EH?

© Steve Bell 1985

STILL ON ROCKALL:

YOU'RE AN **IMPRESSIVE CHAP**, **MIDDLETAR** — COME WITH ME, I THINK YOU SHOULD MEET THE **MEMSAHIB**.... ...OF COURSE YOU'LL HAVE TO MAKE YOURSELF **DECENT** FIRST!

I **THANK THE LORD** THAT I MANAGED TO PRESERVE THIS **FLAG** FROM THE **WRECK OF THE 'PENIS'**, SIR!

GOOD SHOW!

© Steve Bell 1985

MARGARET — I'D LIKE YOU TO MEET A **HERO** — **MIDDLETAR** R.N. CAPTAIN OF H.M.S. **'PENIS'!!**

AT YOUR SERVICE, MA'AM!

NOT THE CAPTAIN OF **THE H.M.S. 'PENIS'**, SURELY?

1101

...WE THOUGHT YOU'D BEEN **BIFFED BY THE REDS**, BUT WE COULDN'T MAKE A **FUSS** BECAUSE...WELL...PEOPLE MIGHT MAKE A STINK IF THEY KNEW A **POLARIS SUB** HAD **GONE MISSING!!**

HAIL, GREAT WHITE METAL MOTHER!!

FAARRP FAARRP BEEP FAARRP BEEP BEEP

IT WAS **VERY DECENT** OF YOU TO LOAN ME YOUR **RAZOR** AND YOUR **HAWAIIAN SHIRT**, MR. **THATCHER**, SIR!

1102.

THINK NOTHING OF IT — MAKE YOURSELF AT HOME!

...WE'VE GOT **EVERYTHING** IN THIS CARAVAN — PORTABLE T.V., VIDEO RECORDER, TAPES, NASTIES...

CROSSROADS — THE MOVIE
CROSSROADS 2
CROSSROADS 3
REVENGE OF CROSSROADS
LIVE AT THE HOUSE OF LORDS
GT. MOMENTS IN DRINKING HISTORY

I **DON'T APPROVE** OF SOME OF THESE PROGRAMMES — DO YOU KNOW THAT SOME-TIMES THEY ACTUALLY **FAIL** TO **READ OUT** THE PRESS **RELEASES** WE TAKE SUCH TROUBLE TO PREPARE?

GOOD LORD! SHAME!!

NEWS

THAT **DAMN** DOG'S SPILT M'DRINK!

OFF! OFF! OFF! OFF!!

DOWN BRITT! THAT'S **ENOUGH**, BOY!!

© Steve Bell 1985

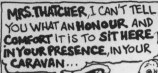 MRS. THATCHER, I CAN'T TELL YOU WHAT AN **HONOUR** AND **COMFORT** IT IS TO SIT HERE IN YOUR PRESENCE, IN YOUR **CARAVAN**...

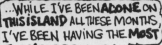 ...WHILE I'VE BEEN **ALONE** ON THIS ISLAND ALL THESE MONTHS, I'VE BEEN HAVING THE **MOST TERRIBLE DREAMS!**

SILLY NONSENSE! Y'KNOW IF I EVER FOUND MYSELF DREAMING, I'D HAVE MYSELF **LOBOTOMISED!**

© Steve Bell 1985

 ANYWAY, WHAT **WERE** THESE TERRIBLE **DREAMS** YOU WERE HAVING? **WHAT WERE THEY ABOUT?**

I KEPT DREAMING THAT I WAS TRAPPED IN A **HUGE BLACK COFFIN** AT THE BOTTOM OF THE OCEAN, **UNABLE TO SPEAK** AND HEARING AN **INSISTENT VOICE** TELLING ME: **YOU ARE BECOME DEATH, MATEY!'**

1105.

GOLLY! WHAT A NASTY DREAM! DON'T WORRY— WE'LL SOON HAVE YOU BACK TO NORMAL DRIVING YOUR **POLARIS** AGAIN!

THANK YOU, MA'AM!

 ANOTHER GOOD THING ABOUT **BRITT** IS HIS **WONDERFULLY ACUTE SENSE OF HEARING** — SEE!! HE'S HEARD **SOMETHING!!**

1106-

 **MICKS!! MICKS!! FENIANS! FENIANS!! FENIANS!!! MICKS! MICKS!! MICKS!!!**

WHAT'S **OUT THERE,** BOY?

 MARGARET'S GOT A **POODLE!** A **FAT DEMENTED POODLE!!**

YOWP? I'M NO POODLE! I'M NO POODLE!!

© Steve Bell 1985

 OF COURSE YOU'RE NOT A **POODLE, BRITT!!** YOU'RE WHAT THE POODLE LEAVES BEHIND ON THE **PAVEMENT!!**

SOMETIMES YOU GET A PRODUCT THAT'S **SO THOROU-GHLY NOXIOUS** YOU WONDER **HOW** THEY COULD **POSSIBLY PROMOTE IT** — BUT THEY DO FIND WAYS. SOMETIMES THE **SHEER INGENUITY** TAKES YOUR BREATH AWAY!

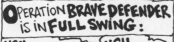

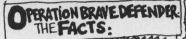 **O**PERATION BRAVE DEFENDER: THE **FACTS**:

THE MAIN REASON FOR THE EXERCISE IS THAT, IN TIME OF WAR WITH RUSSIA...

...MOST BRITISH TROOPS WILL BE OVER IN GERMANY LEAVING VITAL INSTALLATIONS IN THIS COUNTRY VULNERABLE TO ATTACK. OPERATION BRAVE DEFENDER AIMS TO TEST...

TESCO

...THE **PREPAREDNESS** AND **EFFECTIVENESS** OF **DAD'S-ARMY-STYLE RESERVISTS**...

...OR **QUAINT OLD PILES** OF **SMOULDERING RADIO-ACTIVE DUST**...

...SO IF YOU FIND YOURSELF **SURROUNDED BY THE MILITARY** IN THE NEXT DAY OR TWO— **DON'T WORRY**, IT'S JUST **GRANDAD HAVING A BIT OF FUN** HAHA HAAAAARRRGTH!!

OPERATION BRAVE DEFENDER: SOME **MORE FACTS**:

IT'S **ALL YOURS**, SIR!!!

SAY THANKS— WHAT'S **THIS BIT** HERE?

THAT'S **EAST ANGLIA!**

GREAT! I RENAME THAT BIT **RONZANIA!** ...AND WHAT'S THAT CUTE LITTLE **TOWN** DOWN **THERE?**...

THAT'S **NORWICH!**

NOT ANY MORE IT'S NOT— FROM NOW ON IT'S **NATOBURG!!!** WHAT ABOUT **THIS LI'L** OLD BIT OF A **PALACE** DOWN IN HERE?

THAT'S THE **HOUSES OF PARLIAMENT**

WELL THAT'S HENCEFORTH GONNA BE MY **PERSONAL HORSE HOUSE**...HEY!!!

THAT **AIN'T NO HORSE HOUSE**— THAT'S A **DESIGNATED CHEMICAL WEAPONS DUMP!**

BUT...BUT... THAT'S MY **POODLE PARLOUR!**

BAGGER ME, MAAGRIT — THE NEWS FROM SUDEFFRIKA IS ENOUGH TO TURN A MAN TO DRINK...SSSSLLLP!!

WHAT'S THET DINIS??

...I SAY — THE NEWS FROM SUDEFFRIKA IS VERY BED....OUR INVISTMENTS!!

SHATTAP DINIS — I'M LISTENING TO THE NEWS FROM HENDSWORTH!!

NYAAH — IT'S ALL THE SAME — DORKIES ON THE RAMPAGE!! WE'VE GOT TO GET REED OF THE BAGGERS!!!

NO, WE LEAVE THEM TO STEW FOR A BEET; THEN THEY CLEAR OFF OF THEIR OWN ACCORD!!!

1117

REMEMBER, DINIS, WE HEF TO OPERITE WITHIN THE MODERATE SENSIBLE AND PROW-GRISSIVE TRADITIONS OF BREETISH RICEISM!

NOW I WANT ALL YOU DARKIE PAUPERS TO PULL YOUR SOCKS UP!!

MARGARET THATCHER IS ON AN ILL-ADVISED TOUR OF THE TROUBLE SPOTS

WHAT A BLEDDY MESS — JIST A MINUTE... WHAT'S THET I SEE??

STOP IT NOW!!

MOANING MINNIES — COME OUT WITH YOUR HANDS IN THE AIR!

...WHY, IT'S A GROUP OF DOK SKINNED YOUTHS SMOKING DRAGS!

— © STEVE BELL 1985 —

...I KNEW DRAGS AND RICE WERE AT THE BOTTOM OF THIS, SO POUR ME A STIFF ONE DINIS, AND LET'S GET AWAY FROM HERE!!!

It's the Right One

48

49

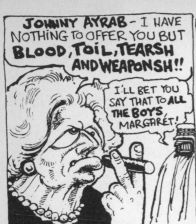

JOHNNY AYRAB - I HAVE NOTHING TO OFFER YOU BUT BLOOD, TOIL, TEARSH AND WEAPONSH!!

I'LL BET YOU SAY THAT TO ALL THE BOYS MARGARET!

1121.

INDEEDIDO, AND I SHAY IT BECAUSHE IT HAPPENSH TO BE TRUE! WEAPONSH ARE THE ONLY GUAR-ANTEED GROWTH INDUSHTRY!

WHAT ABOUT FOOD? SHADDAP!!

THAT ISH WHY I EMPLOY TIT FOR TAT YOYO PINGPONG DIPLOMASHY AND ARDENTLY SHUPPORT SHTAR WARSH!!

I DON'T QUITE SEE, MARGARET?

BECAUSHE, I ASHK YOU - WHO ISH GOING TO BUY WEAPONSH IF THERE ISH A THREAT OF WORLD PEASHE??

© STEVE BELL 1985

DOZO - WHATSH HAPPENING ON THE TIT FOR TAT YOYO PINGPONG EXPULSIONSH FRONT??

1122

WELL...ER... MARGARET... ZZZZZ

I THINK WE'VE GONE ABOUT AS FAR AS WE CAN ON THAT ONE, MARGARET, SNORE...

NONSHENSHE!!! WE MUSHT KEEP THE HEAT UP!! WE MUSHT OUT-FASHE THE EVIL ONE!!

© Steve Bell '85

..BUT..BUT..MARGARET - PEOPLE ARE ALREADY BEGINNING TO WONDER WHY, IF THAT CHAPPIE DEF-ECTED IN JULY, WE SHOULD LEAVE IT UNTIL NOW TO MAKE SUCH A FUSS!?

GRRRR!

CHEW CHEW

PAH! HOW DARE THEY!! DON'T THE TRAITORSH REALISHE THAT REASHONSH OF SHTATE PUBLISHITY MUSHT REIGN SHUPREME?

HOT DAMN! THIS HIGH-FIBRE DIET HAS BEEN DOIN' ME ONE HECK OF A POWER OF GOOD!! CHOFF CHOFF!!

I MAY BE A PUPPET OF BIG BISHNESH, THE BANKSH THE BOMB LOBBY MORL MAJORD'Y AND DISNEYCORP ®™ ....

SKRAWK CHOF

I MAY NOT HAVE A CONSHIOUSH MIND O' MY OWN, AND I MAY BE JUSHT A BIG PIESHE O' WOOD, BUT IT DON'T MATTER!!!

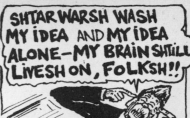

SHTAR WARSH WASH MY IDEA AND MY IDEA ALONE — MY BRAIN SHTILL LIVESH ON, FOLKSH!!

KAPHARRT!!

HEY BOYS!! I'M GONNA HELP THE NEEDY, SO COME 'N' GET YO' FREE STARWARS MEGABUCKS!!

RON! RON! DON'T FORGET ME! IT'S MARGARET — YOUR NUMBER ONE FAITHFUL ALLY!!

OH.. ER.. YEAH? YOU WANNA PIECE O' THE ACTION, HUH?!

PAF!

BAM

HOW'S THAT, MARGARET?

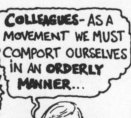

THE AFTERMATH OF THE BELGRAVIA RIOTS.

YES, THESE YOUNG PEOPLE HAVE JUST GOT TOO MUCH MONEY...!!

1133

...YOU SEE THAT LARGE GROUP OVER THERE? DO YOU REALISE THAT ONLY ONE OF THOSE KIDS HAS EVER BEEN ABLE TO HOLD DOWN A JOB FOR MORE THAN A DAY AND A HALF?

...AND DO YOU SEE THIS ONE APPROACHING US NOW? D'YOU MEAN - THE ONE CLUTCHING THE PIMMS BOMB?? YES - DO YOU REAL--ISE THAT HE OWNS ONE FIFTH OF BEDFORDSHIRE? IT'S TOO MUCH TO EXPECT OF A NICE YOUNG CHAP!!

BURNING INNER LUTON TONIGHT!

©Steve Bell '85

BELGRAVIA :- THE AFTERMATH :

NOW I'M ACTUALLY GOING TO INTERVIEW ONE OF THE PARTICIPANTS IN THE SW1 RIOT - THE HON. ALGERNON UPCRUST SPENSIVE-WARDRABE D'ARTY FFARQUAR :-

YAH?

MR. FFARQUAR - IS IT TRUE YOU OWN ONE FIFTH OF BEDFORD-SHIRE??

YAH - THREE FIFTHS, EKSHLY...

©Steve Bell 1985

WELL - WHY? WHY HAVE YOU DESTROYED ALL THESE BUILDINGS??

TOO MUCH PRESSURE - -CAN'T CAPE WITH ALL THE MONEY - -NEED MORE AKYNETANTS!!

...BUT...BUT...WHAT SPARKED IT OFF??

EKSHLY IT WAS ROY HATTERSLEY!

1134

WHAT DO YOU MEAN — 'ROY HATTERSLEY SPARKED OFF THE BELGRAVIA RIOTS??'

UH HUH, YAH, THAT'S EPSLUTE FACT!!

YOU CAN'T BE SERIOUS? YOU MEAN HIS PROPOSALS TO MILDLY MODIFY UPPER TAX BRACKETS??!

YAH! YAH! TOO MUCH PRESSURE! WE SIMPLY HAD TO GO ITE AND PIMMS BOMB A SAYSHLIST, SO WE RAN DINE BARKINGHAM PALACE RAID....

YAH, YAH!

YAH, YAH! THEN WE SAW THESE CHAPS IN RED UNIFORMS

YOU MEAN — CHANGING THE GUARD?

YAH — NAKED SAYSHLIST PROVOCATION! TOO MUCH PRESSURE! — BEEN BUILDING UP FOR EPSLUTELY YAAAARS!!

...I TELL YOU SOMETHING — IF THEY GO ON POURING MONEY INTO THIS AREA THE WAY THEY HAVE BEEN — IT'S GAING TO HAPPEN AGAIN!!

©Steve Bell 1985

DOUGLAS HURD IS TOURING THE S.W.1 TROUBLE SPOTS:

APPALLING, APPALLING, I'M SHOCKED!

COOEE! DOUGLAS!!

GOOD LORD!! HELLO RUPERT! HELLO JULIA!

HELLAY DOUGLAS — HIZE THE FEMLAY??

FINE, THANKS JULIA..... OH...HI JASPER! HI CHARLOTTE!!

'LAY DOUGLAS, HI ZIT GAING?

©Steve Bell 85

QUITE WELL THANKS, JASPER — HOW'S YOUR MOTHER THE COUNTESS?

A.K. EKSHLY DOUGLAS. I SAY — YOU WOULDN'T LIKE TO CALL YOUR CHAPS ORFF, WOULD YOU??

OF COURSE — CONSTABLE — PUT THE VISCOUNT DOWN PLEASE

A PRESS CONFERENCE AT METROPOLITAN POLICE H.Q.

WE HAVE RECEIVED INFORMATION THAT **AGITATORS** OF A **TROTSKYITE** AND **ANARCHISTIC TENDENCY** HAVE ENTERED THE AREA AND ARE INFLUENCING **GULLIBLE YOUTH**

© Steve Bell 1985

PARDON ME, COMMISSIONER—BUT ISN'T THAT RATHER LIKE SAYING THERE ARE **AGITATORS** OF A **CATHOLIC ORANGEMAN TENDENCY**? AREN'T THE TWO **MUTUALLY INCOMPATIBLE**?

1137

NEXT QUESTION?

COMMISSIONER—IN VIEW OF THE CURRENT SITUATION—WHY AREN'T YOU USING **PLASTIC BULLETS** YET? IS THIS NOT DERELICTION OF DUTY ON YOUR PART?

BBC/MI5 PLANT

WORR! YEAH!!

NICE ONE!!

COR—THAT'S A GOOD IDEA, THUNDERCLAP—LET'S GO OUT AND GIVE 'EM A BIT O' **SERIOUS WALLOP!!**

SMAK!!

A BINGO-ITE MONETARIST AGITATOR STALKS THE STREETS OF THE METROPOLIS:

FISH 'N' CHIPS

NEWS 'N' NICK NACKS

—1138.

I WAS UNEMPLOYED—I DIDN'T RIOT!—I JUST CALLED ON A **WEALTHY FRIEND**....

© Steve Bell 1985

...THEN I JUST **SAT DOWN** AND WROTE A BEST SELLER—THAT'S WHAT I DID!!!

SNAX 'N' SEX

BOOKS 'N' BILGE

JEFFREY ARCHER
NOT A PENNY MORE NOT A PENNY LESS
CHUNKY FORMAT COFFEE TABLE EDITION

ARCHER NOT A PENNY MORE NOT A PENNY LESS

CARLOADS OF BINGOITE MONETARIST AGITATORS CONGREGATE AT AN ADDRESS IN CENTRAL LONDON:

NOT A DOORWEDGE MORE NOT A DOOR WEDGE LESS!!

Bingoite Gaffer GENERAL LOCKOUT NOW!!

© Steve Bell · 1985

WHERE'S CECIL? I NEED CECIL!!

HE'S GONE UNDERGROUND, MAG!!

1139

YOU DON'T NEED CECIL, MA'AM— HE'S BEEN PROVED UNWORTHY OF YOU, MA'AM!!!

BUGGER ORFF, GUMMER— I THOUGHT I TOLD YOU YOU'D BEEN PURGED!!

WHAT'S IT ALL ABOUT, EH? WHAT'S IT ALL ABOUT?

I SHOULD COCO—YOU TELL ME, JOHN?

© Steve Bell 1985

IT'S A GAME, EH? YOU SEEN ANY AGITATORS LATELY?

NOT PERSONALLY, NO, JOHN

1140

YOU WOULDN'T HAPPEN TO BE ONE WOULD YOU?

NO WAY. ON YOUR BIKE, YOU!!

TROTSKYIST ANARCHIST!!

TROTSKYIST ANARCHIST!!

TROTSKYIST ANARCHIST WE MUST SWEEP OURSELVES OUT WITH AN IRON BROOM

SOME OF THESE BASTARDS ARE CLEVER THOUGH...

PSSSST... 'ERE MATE— D'YOU WANNA BUY A VAN LOAD O' PLASTIC BULLETS??

61

THEN YOU HAVE THE WHOLE GAMUT OF DIFFERENT SALES METHODS. ONE TECHNIQUE STRIKES ME IN PARTICULAR...

An irate cartoon character speaks out:

I ASK YOU THIS:

HOW WOULD YOU LIKE IT IF THE LIMITS OF YOUR ENTIRE UNIVERSE WERE SUDDENLY REDUCED BY 20%??

IT MAKES YOU FEEL PRETTY SMALL——I KNOW—I WAS HATCHED ON THIS STRIP!!

© Steve Bell 1985

AND WHY HAS THIS COME ABOUT?? SO CROSSWORD BUFFS CAN HAVE SOME BLANK SPACE FOR DOODLING IN!!

WELL—WHAT ABOUT THE SHORT SIGHTED PUNTERS TRYING TO READ THIS LOT OVER HERE??

I'VE JUST GOT ONE THING TO SAY: IF YOU WANT TO DOODLE—GO OUT AND BUY A BLOODY DOODLE PAD!!

1147

...AND ANOTHER THING——I'VE GOT ANOTHER EGG ON THE WAY AND I CARE PASSIONATELY ABOUT THE SORT OF ENVIRONMENT I WANT MY OFFSPRING BROUGHT UP IN!!...

© Steve Bell 1985

...I DON'T WANT IT POLLUTED WITH NUCLEAR WASTE, I DON'T WANT IT STACKED UP WITH BOMBS AND I DON'T WANT IT SHRUNK! OKAY?

1148

ALRIGHT, BONEHEAD——YOU CAN HAVE YOUR EPISODE BACK NOW. COME, PRUDENCE!

HARRUMMPH!!

IN THE MASONS 🎵 IN THE MASONS 🎵

IT'S A GAME, EH?

WHERE ARE WE, PHILLIP??

— © Steve Bell 1985 —

I DAYN'T KNAY— —I THINK WE'RE SOMEWHERE IN THE CARIBBEAN

WHO'S THE FET LITTLE CHEP IN THE FINERY??

DAYN'T KNAY— —COULD BE A FLUNKEY, COULD BE A HEAD OF STATE. ONE NEVER CAN TELL WITH THESE TYPES!

1155

HELLAY!

TAKE ME TO YOUR LEADER— —DO YOU COME HERE ORFTEN? MILD FOR THE TIME OF YAHR, ISN'T IT? DO YOU PEOPLE EAT RETS TOO??

IT IS OVER THIRTY YAHRS SINCE I LAST VISITED THIS LARVELY ISLAND....

— © Steve Bell 1985 —

SINCE THET TIME, MY OWN FEMLAY HAS GRAYN, AS, I AM SURE HAVE YOUR OWN FEMLAYS...

THERE, HYEVER, THE SIMILARITY ENDS— —BECAUSE I PERSONALLY AM A MONARCH WITH A VAIR VAIR HIGH INCOME. YOU PEOPLE I AM AFRAID ARE NOT...

...WHICH IS WHY YOU MAST NOT LET THE GRAYTH IN YOUR POPULATION ITESTRIP THE CREATION OF JORBS..

BRAVAY!

TELL IT LIKE IT IS!!

1156

"OH BRIXTON HILL IS THE PLACE TO BE...

...ON THE BANKS OF THE A23....

NO SANDY BEACHES OR HUMMING BIRD...

...JUST COMMUNITY SNATCH SQUADS AND DOUGLAS HURD"

"NOW RONALD REAGAN IS WILD AND FREE WITH A PECULIAR GRIP ON REALITY HE'D HAVE YOU THINK HE IS STATELY + WISE BUT HE'S MUCH TOO FOND OF HIS OWN PORK PIES...

TWO YEARS AGO IN THE LEBANON RON JUMPED ITE OF THE FIRE INTO THE FRYING PAN WITH THE DIPLOMACY OF A KISSINGER FAN RON STARTED SHELLING CIVILIAN....

..BUT 200 MARINES BLEW TO KINGDOM COME WHICH DIDN'T ENDEAR RON TO THE FOLKS BACK HOME HE WAS LOOKIN' FAIRLY USELESS AND DUMB TILL HE LANCED GRENADA LIKE A BOIL ON HIS BUM...

..SO REMEMBER THIS MORAL AND RECEIVE IT WITH THANKS IF YOU'VE GOT DISSENSION WITHIN YOUR RANKS YOU MUST SEND IN THE TROOPS YOU MUST SEND IN THE TANKS TWO YEARS LATER SEND ME ROUND OPENING BANKS!"

GAND BLESS THIS ENORMOUS BENK AND ALL WHO FAIL IN HER...

74

WE'RE COMIN' FOR YOU, GORBACHEV!!

© Steve Bell 1985

...THE STOCKPILED HAIRSTYLES OF THE ENTIRE WESTERN ALLIANCE ARE ON THEIR WAY!

WORLD WAR THREE IS GONNA BE ABOUT PRESENTATION...

NOBODY IS GOING TO GIVE A SHIT WHO WINS SO LONG AS WHOEVER IT IS LOOKS GOOD WHEN IT'S ALL OVER!

1165

MR PRESIDENT — IS YOUR HAIR COMPLETELY UNDER CONTROL?

YUP!

THE BIG SUMMIT

MR PRESIDENT, WE DON'T WANT YOU TO GO IN THERE UNLESS YOU ARE COMPLETELY CONFIDENT THAT YOUR HAIR IS NOT GOING TO DECLARE WAR OF ITS OWN ACCORD!

NOPE!

OKAY! GO FOR IT MR PRESIDENT, GO FOR IT!!

1166

SHOVE

MY GODDAMN HAIR DEFECTED!!

© Steve Bell 1985

THE BIG SUMMIT

H.M. GOVERNMENT WARNING: THERE MAY BE SOME SLIGHT HEALTH RISK INVOLVED IN A POLICY OF ALL OUT TIT FOR TAT TOTAL INTERSTELLAR MEGADEATH, BUT WHO'S WORRYING?

THEN YOU GET THE **PECULIAR ABSTRACT ONES**, WHERE THE ONLY OBVIOUS MESSAGE APPEARS TO BE THE **HEALTH WARNING** AT THE **BOTTOM**....THESE ONES **REALLY GET ON MY TITS!**

H.M. GOVERNMENT HEALTH WARNING: DYING OF LUNG CANCER CAN REALLY FUCK YOU UP

I WANT MY HAIR BACK—NOW!!

NYET

I CAN'T THINK SHTRAIGHT WITHOUT MY HAIR!!

HO HO HO!

YOU SHTINKIN' SHOVIET SHTOOGE!! YOU SHTOLE MY HAIR AWAY!!!

NUTS!! I CAME O' MY OWN FREE WILL!!

AND TO PROVE IT I'M GONNA CALL A PRESS CONFERENCE

OH MY GAHD!!

HO HO HO

© Steve Bell '85

1164

RONALD REAGAN'S DEFECTING HAIR IS GIVING A PRESS CONFERENCE......

I CAME OVER TO THE SOVIETS OF MY OWN ACCORD....

...FOR YEARS I HAD BEEN SUBJECTED TO THE MOST CRUDE FORMS OF BRAINWASHING THROUGH CONSTANT FORCED EXPOSURE TO THE DIREST EXTREMES OF REACT-IONARY IDEOLOGY...

1168

...THEN IN RECENT YEARS I WAS SUBJECTED TO A MERCILESS REGIME OF CHEMICAL TORTURE...

© Steve Bell 1985

...I WAS FORCED, TOTALLY AGAINST MY WILL TO ABSORB MANY MANY GALLONS OF GRECIAN 2000!

80

MR PRESIDENT— —WE HAVE BROUGHT BACK YOUR HAIR!

GIMME!!

GIMME GIMME GIMME NOW!!

HEY! WHAT'SH GOIN' ON HERE? THISH DOESHN'T FEEL LIKE MY HAIR— THISH FEELSH LIKE DULL LIFELESSH PROBLEM HAIR!!

WE WERE FORCED TO TERMINATE WITH EXTREME PREJUDICE, SIR!

I DON'T CARE ABOUT THAT SHIT—I WANNA KNOW WHAT'S HAPPENED TO MY POINTY BIT!!

1171.

WELL YURI.... ...AWW SURE, MIKHAIL— —THIS HAS BEEN A REALLY WORTHWHILE EXPERIENCE... ...SNIFF... SNIFF...

MIKHAIL!

HO HO HO!

OH SHIT, AWW JEEZ!! MY HAIR! MY POOR DEAD HAIR!! SOB, CHOKE, OH GAHD! OH GAHD! OUTFACED BY A BALD COMMIE WITH A SKIDMARK ON HIS HEAD!! SOB, GROAN, WAAAAHH!!

FLOP

© STEVE BELL 1985

I'VE BEEN A SUCKER YURI...MIKHAIL..... ..Y'KNOW...I'M NO LINGUIST, BUT...

...I DON'T THINK THE RUSSIAN LANGUAGE HAS A WORD FOR "BRAINLESS BOZO FRONTMAN FOR A PSYCHOTIC RIGHT- -WING PRESSURE GROUP"!?

1172.

IN YOUR DREAMS YOU'VE BEEN TO

ROCKALL

AND JUST **WHAT GOES** ON IN ROCKALL?

1173.

I'LL TELL YOU— ABSOLUTELY F*** ALL, MATEY!!

YOU'RE TURNING INTO A **CYNIC** AND A **WASTER!!!** THERE'S NOTHING WRONG WITH THIS PLACE—THIS IS A **VIABLE SOCIALIST SEABIRD COMMUNITY!!**

GLUG

COD LIVER OIL

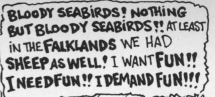

BLOODY SEABIRDS! NOTHING BUT BLOODY SEABIRDS!! AT LEAST IN THE FALKLANDS WE HAD SHEEP AS WELL! I WANT **FUN!!** I NEED **FUN!!** I DEMAND **FUN!!!**

COD LIVER OIL

© Steve Bell '85

YOU WANT **FUN??** WHAT DO YOU THINK **I** WANT? I WANT **FUN** TOO! EVERYBODY WANTS **FUN**, MATEY!!

I'D LIKE SOME FUN!!

I'M ENTITLED TO FUN, ME!!

COD LIVER OIL

WHAT'S FUN THEN?? **WHAT IS FUN??** THERE'S **MORE** TO **FUN** THAN **SNACKS** AND **FISH OIL** MATEY!!!

1174.

WHAT DO YOU MEAN? I DON'T DRINK A LOT!!

SO, I LIKE THE OCCAS-IONAL COD LIVER OIL OF AN EVENING (GULP) AND THE ODD **SCAMPI-FRY-STYLE-SNACK-SO WHAT?**

SO, IT'S THE MIDDLE OF THE MORNING AND YOU'RE ALREADY **BLOTTO!!**

© Steve Bell '85

GIVE ME THAT BOTTLE !!!

GLORIA! GLORIA!! NOT IN YOUR CONDITION SURELY??

SHADDAP! (GULP)

SNATCH

82

83

PRUDENCE, PENGUIN SEXUALITY IS A MANY-FACETED AND WONDROUS THING!! TAKE FOR EXAMPLE THE REPRODUCTIVE CYCLE OF THE BIG PENGUINS:

1177

...THE FEMALE EMPEROR PENGUIN PRODUCES ONE EGG IN THE LATE AUTUMN WHICH SHE IMMEDIATELY HANDS OVER TO THE MALE TO INCUBATE WHILE SHE GOES AND HAS FUN...

THE MALES THEN SIT FOR WEEKS THROUGH TERRIBLE BLIZZARDS, HUDDLED IN LARGE GROUPS. WHEN THE EGG HATCHES, THE FEMALES RETURN AND TAKE OVER FOR ANOTHER FEW WEEKS, WHILE THE MALES GO OFF AND HAVE FUN, AND SO IT GOES ON....

...PRUDENCE - BIG PENGUINS ARE GAY BY CUSTOM AND BY CHOICE, AND WE'RE PROUD OF IT TOO!!

© Steve Bell 1985

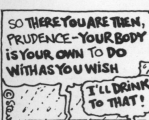

SO THERE YOU ARE THEN, PRUDENCE - YOUR BODY IS YOUR OWN TO DO WITH AS YOU WISH

I'LL DRINK TO THAT!

© Steve Bell 1985

HAVE FUN WITH IT OR NOT, AS YOU WISH - YOU CAN'T IMPOSE FUN ON OTHERS, NOR CAN THEY IMPOSE IT ON YOU. I'VE ONLY ONE PIECE OF MOTHERLY ADVICE TO OFFER YOU:

1178

IF IT FEELS GOOD IF IT FEELS GOOD - DO IT!! - DO IT!!!

BOING!! BOING!

BOING!!

DO IT!! - DO IT!!!! DO IT!!!

BOING!!

GLORIA! IS THIS WISE IN YOUR CONDITION?

84

BREAKFAST TIME AT THE HOME OF THE **NEWLY REBUILT** MARGARET THATCHER

MARGARET—WE'RE **UP THE CREEK!** — WHAT ARE YOU TALKING ABOUT? YOUR **SIX BILLION DOLLAR REFIT**— IT'S **BANKRUPTED US!!!**

SSSSSLLP

THE THATCHER BREAKFAST— BLACK COFFEE AND A VITAMIN 'C' TABLET

ALL OUR **SOUTH AFRICAN HOLDING**, ALL SALARIES + FEES FOR THE **REST OF THE CENTURY**, EVERY SINGLE **POSSESSION, GONE!!**

ARE YOU **SURE ABOUT THIS??**

SLURP

FOAM FIZZ

WHAT ABOUT OUR **BARRATT HOME ??**

A TREE FELL ON IT!! APART FROM WHAT'S IN THIS GIN BOTTLE WE HAVE **ABSOLUTELY NO LIQUID ASSETS!!**

WE NEED **CASH IN HAND**, MARGARET— I'M AFRAID **YOU KNOW WHAT THIS MEANS, DON'T YOU??** — YOU MEAN?. YES—ONE OF US HAS GOT TO GO AND **QUEUE UP AT THE POST OFFICE!!**

Pension or allowance

BANKRUPTED BY A **SIX BILLION DOLLAR** REPAIR BILL, THE **THATCHERS** ARE FORCED TO **QUEUE UP** AT THE **POST OFFICE:**

I FAIL TO SEE WHY A **BIONIC WORLD LEADER** SHOULD HAVE TO DO **THIS!!** WE NEED THE **CASH, MAG**

1182.

GIVE ME MY OLD AGE PENSION **NOW!** DO YOU REALISE **WHO I AM??!?**

BOING!

WHAT'S THIS? **JOKE MONEY?** I SAY, DENIS— —IT'S A DAMNED GOOD JOB WE HAVE THE **FREE HOUSE** AND THE **FREE DINNERS!!**

SHIVER & SHAKE

DO YOU REALISE THIS ISN'T GOING TO BE ENOUGH TO EVEN COPE WITH YOUR **G+T. HABIT?**

AAAAARRGH!!

88

DENIS HAS TAKEN OVER AS ARCHBISHOP OF CANTERBURY:

PRETTY NIFTY LITTLE OFFICE, MARGARET! (GLUG)..

1189.

I THINK WE COULD DO WITH A FEW MINOR DECOR CHANGES HERE, DENIS

WHATEVER YOU WANT OLD GIRL

AH YES— —SO MUCH MORE UPLIFTING!

...WE HAVE TO BRING PEOPLE BACK TO THE FAITH - WE NEED MORE FUNNY CLOTHES, MORE INCOMPREHENSIBLE LITURGICAL CLAPTRAP; AND THERE'S ONE OTHER THING WHICH HAS TO BE A CLINCHER....

1190.

...I'M TALKING ABOUT LIVE MUSIC, DENIS!

SLUMP-SLUMP BOOM BOOM SLUMP...

TISH TISH TATISH

NORMAN TEBBIT AND HIS UNPERMISSIVE STONE COLD STIFF ARSED PREWAR NON FUNKING FIVE

© Steve Bell 1985

Panel 1:
I DON'T BELIEVE IT!! HOW CAN THEY BE SO STUPID??
1191.
WE MUST PURGE PURGE AND PURGE AGAIN!

Panel 2:
WE MUST URGENTLY PURGE THE SURGING MILITANT SCOURGE!
AGAGAG YIBBLE YIBBLE YIN YIN YIN!!

Panel 3:
THAT'S IT! ENOUGH IS ENOUGH! I'VE CRACKED! I CAN'T TAKE ANY MORE OF THIS CRAP!!
WE MUST BLAST AWAY THE CANCEROUS FLUFF FROM OUR NAVELS WITH AN EARNEST FLAME-THROWER
SNAP!!

Panel 4:
THE STUPID BALD GIT!! I WANNA STRANGLE HIM! I WANNA STRANGLE HIM!!
EASY, JOHN - HE IS THE LEADER AFTER ALL... AND THERE'S NO NEED TO BE HAIRIST!

Panel 5:
THE AGM OF INNER LONDON WILDLIFE FOR LABOUR:
I NOW CALL UPON COLLEAGUE JOHN THE MONKEY TO SPEAK ON THE MOTION....

Panel 6:
FRIENDS, COMRADES, FELLOW CREATURES - THE MOTION BEFORE US PROPOSES THAT INNER LONDON WILDLIFE SHOULD RESOLUTELY SUPPORT ANYTHING COLLEAGUES KINNERSLEY-HADDOCK SHOULD THINK FIT IN ORDER TO WIN THE NEXT ELECTION.

1192

Panel 7:
BUT BEFORE I SAY ANYTHING SPECIFIC ABOUT THE MOTION, I'D LIKE TO TELL YOU A PARABLE. YOU'VE PROBABLY HEARD THE ONE ABOUT THE EMPEROR'S NEW CLOTHES?

Panel 8:
WELL, THIS ONE IS ABOUT THE WOULD-BE-EMPEROR'S CLOTHES PHOBIA!!

93

THE INNER LONDON WILDLIFE A.G.M.

ONCE UPON A TIME IN A LAND RULED BY A **CRUEL** AND **CORRUPT EMPRESS**...

...THERE LIVED A **WOULD-BE EMPEROR** WHO LOVED TO **PARADE AROUND THE TOWN**. HE HAD A **FINE SUIT OF CLOTHES**, AND WANTED **EVERYONE** TO HAVE CLOTHES AS **FINE** AS **HIS**...

...AND HE WANTED TO **SHARE THE EXPERIENCE** OF HAVING SUCH **TRULY FINE CLOTHES**, SO **EVERY DAY** HE WOULD GO AROUND **TELLING THE WHOLE TOWN** ABOUT HIS CLOTHES...

1193.

ALL DAY HE WOULD DESCRIBE HIS CLOTHES IN **FULSOME PHRASES**. UNFORTUNATELY HE NEVER ACTUALLY **GOT AROUND** TO **PUTTING** THEM ON.

AS THE **WOULD-BE EMPEROR** PARADED AROUND THE TOWN, HE DID HIS BEST TO **IGNORE** THE **MALEVOLENT TOWN CRIERS** WHO, INSTEAD OF **PROMOTING** HIS **TRULY FINE CLOTHES**, AS HE WOULD HAVE **WISHED**...

...INSISTED ON BELLOWING:

HEAR YE! HEAR YE!!! PLAGUE-RIDDEN PERVERT STILL AT LARGE HORROR!!!

...FOR THEY WERE **ALL** IN THE **PAY** OF THE **CRUEL EMPRESS**, WHO, INCIDENTALLY WAS NOT ONLY **COMPLETELY STARK NAKED HERSELF**....

1194.

...BUT ALSO RODE AROUND IN AN **ARMOUR-PLATED BARREL** ON A **GIGANTIC COCKROACH** WITH A LARGE RETINUE OF DISEASE - **CARRYING FLEAS!**

HEAR YE!! BEST DRESSED EMPRESS IN HEALTH TRIUMPH FOR BRITAIN!

94

THE WOULD·BE·EMPEROR WAS VERY UPSET AT WHAT THE MALEVOLENT TOWN CRIERS WERE SAYING ABOUT HIM...

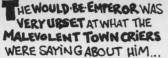

HEAR YE! HEAR YE!! PLAGUE·RIDDEN PERVERT HAS POX SHOCK!!

..AND TO MAKE MATTERS WORSE HE BEGAN TO FEEL AN ITCH IN THE REGION OF HIS GROIN. HE RESOLVED TO TAKE CHARGE OF THE SITUATION...

HEAR YE! HEAR YE! PLAGUE PERVERT IN SOCIAL DISEASE DRAMA!

© Steve Bell 1985

..THE VERY NEXT DAY HE STEPPED OUT, STILL WITHOUT ANY CLOTHES ON, AND MARCHED TO THE TOWN SQUARE. HE SEIZED THE BELL OFF A PASSING TOWN CRIER AND BEGAN TO RING IT VIGOROUSLY...

1195

..WHEN A CROWD HAD GATHERED, HE JUMPED ON AN ORANGE BOX, POINTED AT HIS GROIN AND BEGAN TO DECLAIM:

SEE! I AM GOING TO PURGE AND SCOURGE THE CRABS FROM MY PRIVATES WITH THIS BUNDLE OF STICKS!!!

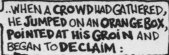

CENSORED IN THE INTERESTS OF PARTY UNITY

"THE WOULD·BE·EMPEROR BEGAN TO SCOURGE HIS LOINS WITH A BUNDLE OF STICKS....

CRABS OUT! CRABS OUT! CRABS OUT!

© Steve Bell 1985

CENSORED IN THE INTERESTS OF PARTY UNITY

LASH

THRASH

SMACK

..THE PEOPLE OF THE TOWN WERE DISMAYED, THOUGH THERE WAS AN ELEMENT AMONGST THE CROWD WHICH, EGGED ON BY THE MALEVOLENT TOWN CRIERS, TOOK UP THE CHANT

1196.

NNNNGGHFFF!!!

CRABS OUT! CRABS OUT! CRABS OUT!

THE WOULD·BE·EMPEROR UNWISELY TOOK THIS AS A SIGN OF POPULAR ACCLAIM AND SMILED WINNINGLY AT THE CROWD....

CRABS OUT!! CRABS OUT!

BUT JUST AT THAT MOMENT THE CRUEL EMPRESS'S PET GIANT PLAGUE VIRUS NORMAN DECIDED TO JOIN IN THE FUN:

CRABS OUT!! CRABS OUT!!

95

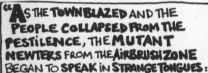

DECADES PASS AND MARGARET THATCHER FACES A NEW CHALLENGE

EXCELLENT - THERE'S NO PROBLEM WITH YOUR VOWELS AND THE NEW HUSKINESS IS COMING ON APACE... ..WE DO HAVE ONE SLIGHT PROBLEM THOUGH....

1201.

SAND + BATTERY ACID GARGLE

YOU MUST APPEAR TO PUT MORE FEELING INTO THE WORDS — —IT'S NOT ENOUGH TO SIMPLY SAY "THE TRAGEDY OF UNEMPLOY-MENT" - ONE HAS TO LOOK AS THOUGH ONE MEANS IT

STIFLED YAWN

...WHICH IS WHY I'M ADVISING YOU TO GET THIS VERY LARGE ONION OUT AT CERTAIN MOOD MOMENTS

GORDON - YOU THINK OF EVERYTHING

©Steve Bell 1985

BWAAHOOOO!!! I'M SO PLEASED!! HOW WOULD YOU LIKE A KNIGHTHOOD, GORDON? BWAHONK SNORT ALDERMAN ROBERTS HOWL!!

1986: THE DUEL OF THE GIANTS.

A 15 ROUND, NO HOLDS-BARRED DEADWEIGHT-POODLE-WRESTLING BOUT BETWEEN, IN THE BLUE CORNER, BATTLER BRITTAN REPRESENTING THE HUGELY LUCRATIVE® KENTUCKY FRIED VULTURE†© FRANCHISE:

Kentucky Fried Vulture

..AND IN THE PUCE CORNER, HERO OF MOLESWORTH— HE-MAN© REPRESENTING THE STONED CROW EURO-BURGER FRANCHISE:

1202. GRUNT

STONED CROW PATRIOTIC EURO-BURGERS

...NOW THE TWO HEROES ARE CIRCLING EACH OTHER WARILY. HE-MAN® HAS ADOPTED HIS FAMOUS POISED-TO-POUNCE POSE...

SNIFF SNIFF

Kentucky Vulture

STONED CROW PATRIOTIC EURO-BURGERS

...AND IT LOOKS LIKE HE-MAN© HAS DONE SOMETHING RATHER UNPLEASANT ON THE CANVAS!!

©Steve Bell 1986

98

THIS IS A **TITANIC DEADWEIGHT** CONTEST BETWEEN **BATTLER BRITTAN**® AND **HE-MAN**© **HESELTINE**®, THE WINNER TO BE DECIDED BY **TWO BACKHANDERS** OR AN **HEREDITARY PEERAGE**...

1203.

...AND BRITTAN IS **DOWN**!!! THE MAN THEY CALL THE **DYNAMO DOG DROPPING** IS ON THE **CANVAS**!!

NNNNN GG MMMPH!!

GRUNT!

STONED CROW PATRIOTIC EURO-BURGERS

—©STEVE BELL 1986—

..BUT **LOOK! HELP** HAS COME FROM AN **UNEXPECTED DIRECTION**. COULD THIS BE A **SETBACK** FOR THE **INDIGENOUS HI-TECH-LETHAL-EURO-BIRD-BURGER INDUSTRY??** ONLY TIME WILL TELL!!

SICKENING CRUNCH

THE **OUTCOME** OF THIS **HUGELY PRINCIPLED STRUGGLE** WILL AFFECT **EVERY ONE** OF US. THE **PRIZE** IS THE **CONTROL OF** BRITAIN'S **LAST** REMAINING **WHIRLING TURKEY FACTORY**...

1204.

...WILL CONTROL FALL INTO THE HANDS OF A **CORPORATE AMERICAN FRANCHISING MONSTER MONOLITH??**

FLIP

SLAM

...OR WILL IT FALL INTO THE HANDS OF A **MONOLITHIC AMERICAN MEGA-MONSTER FRANCHISING CORPORATION??** ONLY TIME WILL TELL!!

©STEVE BELL 1986

THE OTHER ONE I LOATHE is the **THINLY VEILED THREAT** TYPE OF AD. THESE AIM TO MAKE YOU **FEEL GUILTY** FOR **NOT HAVING** SOMETHING THAT YOU **DON'T WANT** AND **DON'T NEED**. INCIDENTALLY, DID YOU KNOW THAT **DOUGLAS HURD** IS RHYMING SLANG FOR WHAT **WE DOGS LEAVE** ON THE **PAVEMENT** ?

101

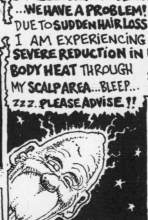

OKAY GEOFFREY-YOUR TURN NOW. SAY SOMETHING YOU KNOW TO BE TRUE

THERE'S NOTHING I LIKE BETTER THAN A REALLY BIG, NO-HOLDS-BARRED, ALL-OUT SNOOZE!

TRUE

PING

...NOW SOMETHING YOU KNOW TO BE FALSE.

I HAVE FELT IT NECESSARY TO JOIN A TRADE UNION THIS WEEK!!

WHAAAT??

TRUE

PING

1215

WHAT'S THIS? IS THERE SOME KIND OF PLOT HATCHING AMONGST MY POODLES, GEOFFREY??

NO! NO!! MARGARET!! IT'S THAT DAMNED MACHINE-IT'S ON THE BLINK! HONESTLY!

LIE

PHTHAAARRP

SWEAT

THE PORKPIE-O-GRAPH® NEVER LIES, HOWE!! THERE'S SOMETHING GOING ON, ISN'T THERE, WORM??

N-N-N-N-O, MARGARET!

IT COULDN'T POSSIBLY MAKE A MISTAKE-IT'S AMERICAN!! IT'S MADE WITH THE LATEST DESIGNER-DRUG-INDUCED WEST COAST SUNRISE TECHNOLOGY, FOOL!

CUCKOO! CUCKOO!

LIE

PPHTHAAARRP!!

1216

MARGARET-YOU CAN'T GO ON TREATING UPPER ECHELON TYPES LIKE MERE G.C.H.Q. STAFFERS...

...YOU MUST ACCEPT THAT WE'RE ALL COMPLETELY CLEAN AND 100 PER CENT ON YOUR SIDE, MA'AM!!!

AH!! THAT'S ALRIGHT THEN GEOFFREY!

LIE, BUT IN THE INTERESTS OF STATE SECURITY

PHTHAAARRP

107

MEANWHILE, ON ROCKALL: GREENHAM WOMEN MAY BE SOVIET SPIES AND MEMBERS OF THE ELITE 'SPETSNAZ' SPECIAL FORCE...

...ACCORDING TO AN ARTICLE IN THE AUTHORITATIVE JANE'S WHIZZ-BANG-POOP-POOP WEEKLY....

HONK! I'M BORED!

KLIK

RIDICULOUS CRAP!! WHO IS THIS JANE?

WHAT DO YOU MEAN 'HONK YOU'RE BORED'??

TOSS

I WANT MONEY AND POWER NOW!!

WHAT'S UP WITH HIM?

IT'S HAPPENED BEFORE-- HE GETS ENORMOUSLY FAT, AND THEN COMES OVER ALL IDEOLOGICALLY UNSOUND!!

WANNA WHEEL & DEAL NOW!!!

TOTTER

© Steve Bell '86

1217

I'M GONNA WHEEL AND DEAL ON THE TURD FUTURES MARKET, AND NOBODY'S GONNA STOP ME!!!

WHAT FOR?

HMS PENIS

I'M GONNA MAKE LOTS OF CASH FOR ME, NOW!!

WHAT DO YOU WANT CASH FOR?

I WANNA BUY FERRARIS AND DOUBLE DINNERS!!

RUB RUB

1218

AND SO, ON THE MARKETS:

HEY! THE TURD'S FIRMING UP ALL OF A SUDDEN!!

IT'S A PETRO-CURRENCY-BOUND TO SOFTEN IN THE LONG TERM!

TURDS? NAH! I'VE HAD THEM BEFORE-- THEY'RE JUST A LOT OF OLD SHIT!!

HE SAYS NO WAY IS IT A PETRO-CURRENCY-- HE SAYS IT'S A BRITISH RAIL CHEESE SANDWICH CURRENCY!!

NOW YOU'RE TALKING!!

DITCH THOSE POUNDS!! INTO TURDS!!

© Steve Bell

Panel 1: WHAT ARE YOU DOING, MAN? / I'VE JUST BOUGHT 20 MILLION BRITISH RAIL CHEESE SANDWICHES AT 37p!!

Panel 2: 20 MILLION? THERE CAN'T BE 20 MILLION BRITISH RAIL CHEESE SANDWICHES IN EXISTENCE — SURELY GOOD SENSE TELLS YOU THAT?? / GABBLER GABBLER JAB JAB PUNCH PUNCH

Panel 3: WHAT'S GOOD SENSE GOT TO DO WITH ANYTHING G??? I'VE JUST SOLD 20 MILLION BRITISH RAIL CHEESE SANDWICHES AT 42p!! I'VE JUST MADE A MILLION QUID IN 45 SECONDS!! / STEAM / ©Steve Bell 1986

Panel 4: WHAT ARE YOU GOING TO DO WITH THESE ILL GOTTEN GAINS? / I'M GONNA BECOME A PRESS BARON!! / DO YOU EVER STOP AND WONDER HOW ALL THIS WILL AFFECT THE BRITISH RAIL CHEESE SANDWICH?? / ·1219·

Panel 5: BACK IN PECKHAM: / COOEE!! HOW'S IT GOING? / GORDON BENNETT!

Panel 6: I'VE JUST COME INTO A LOAD OF MONEY, I'VE SEEN THE LIGHT AND I WANT TO START A NEWSPAPER!! / YOU'VE BEEN PUTTING IT ON, HAVEN'T YOU??

Panel 7: YOU'RE GOING THROUGH ONE OF YOUR HUGELY OVERWEIGHT, IDEOLOGICALLY RETROGRADE PHASES, AREN'T YOU?? / ME? NO! I'VE JUST COME TO RECOGNISE ONE OR TWO COMMERCIAL REALITIES, THAT'S ALL! / ·220·

Panel 8: YEAH, LIKE WHAT? / WELL, LIKE THE NEED FOR PUBLIC SECTOR CUTS, GENERAL PAY RESTRAINT, AND THE NEED FOR MAXIMISED GROSS CASH FOR ME PERSONALLY NOW!!! / ©Steve Bell 1986

SO YOU'RE GOING TO **START A NEWSPAPER** AND **TELL THE WORLD** ABOUT YOUR **STARTLING NEW DISCOVERY**, ARE YOU??

YUP! YOU SEE, WITH THE NEW **LO·STAFF, LO·COST, FLEXIBLE, EFFICIENT PRINTING TECHNOLOGY** IT'S SO MUCH **EASIER** TO **START ONE UP!!**

© Steve Bell 1986

THE **POTENTIAL** FOR **NEW EXCITING** PAPERS OF **ALL SHADES OF OPINION** HAS **NEVER BEEN GREATER!**

WHAT ABOUT **MONEY?**

IT'S **EASY** TO GET **MONEY!**

OH REALLY? LISTEN— I'VE GOT AN **IDEA**— —LET'S DO AN **EXPERIMENT!**

BOOST BOOST GLEAM GLEAM

LET'S **BOTH** TRY AND **START A NEWSPAPER**; YOU START ONE TO PROPOUND YOUR NEW, **POSITIVE COMMERCIALLY VIABLE PHILOSOPHY**, AND I'LL START ONE TO PROPOUND MY **SOCIALISTIC, ANIMALISTIC PHILOSOPHY**, O.K?

...BUT WE HAVE TO **START FROM SCRATCH** AND **RAISE ALL THE MONEY** FROM **LIKELY SOURCES:**

HELLO? IS THAT **LAZARUS DUMBRO MERCHANT BANKERS? CAPITAL! CAPITAL!**

HELLO? IS THAT THE **G.L.C?**

1221

MY **NEW PAPER** IS GOING TO BE CALLED '**NEWTURDAY**' IT'S GOING TO BE **FLEXIBLE, EFFICIENT, CLEAN, COLOURFUL, POSITIVE, NEW** AND **EXCITING**, YET IT'S GOING TO BE **FIRMLY ANCHORED** IN **SOLID, TRADITIONAL VALUES**

...**VALUES** LIKE FUNDAMENTAL **FREEDOM FOR MONEY**, THE **BASIC HUMAN RIGHT TO MANAGE**, THE **RIGHT TO OBEY THE POLICE**, AND THE **NEED FOR TITS, BUMS** AND REALLY RACY DRIVEL ABOUT **LIFESTYLES 'N' GOSSIP!!** POLITICALLY IT WILL BE IN THE **MIDDLE OF THE ROAD TO OBLIVION**, AND I'VE ALREADY **RAISED £3 MILLION!!**

© Steve Bell 1986

MY **PAPER** IS GOING TO BE CALLED '**THE CREATURE**' IT'S GOING TO BE **FLEXIBLE, EFFICIENT, CLEAN, COLOURFUL, LOOK NEW AND EXCITING** etc. etc. IT'S GOING TO BE **FIRMLY ANCHORED** IN **SOLID TRADITIONAL VALUES**....

1222.

...LIKE **PEACE, SOCIAL JUSTICE, PRODUCTION FOR NEED NOT PROFIT, FREEDOM FROM FEAR** AND FROM **HUNGER** IT WILL BE **OWNED** AND **CONTROLLED BY THOSE WHO WORK ON IT**. POLITICALLY IT WILL **STAND ON THE LEFT**, AND I'VE ALREADY **RAISED MINUS £4·32p**

OKAY — YOU'VE GOT THE MONEY TO START A PAPER — BUT WHO ARE YOU GOING TO GET TO WORK ON IT?

I'LL GET WORKERS WHO RESPECT MY FUNDAMENTAL HUMAN RIGHT TO MANAGE!

I WANT WORKERS WHO WILL JUMP WHEN I SAY JUMP; I WANT WORKERS WHO WILL SIGN LEGALLY BINDING AGREEMENTS TO OBEY MY EVERY WHIM!!

PANT
PANT

© Steve Bell 1986

WHO ON EARTH ARE YOU GOING TO GET TO AGREE TO ALL THAT?

SIMPLE — I'LL USE HIGHLY TRAINED DOGS!!

EAGER ELECTRIC TRAINEE POODLEE UNION

1223

OKAY BOYS: LESSON ONE: GOING TO WORK: STAGE ONE:

© Steve Bell 1986

'PUTTING YOUR COLOUR CODED COLLAR ON IN THE DARK'

STAGE TWO: 'GETTING IN THE BUS' NOW REMEMBER: NO BARKING, NO HOWLING, NO COCKING YOUR LEG, AND MOST DEFINITELY NONE OF THAT!!

1224

STAGE THREE: QUIETLY TRAVELLING TO YOUR LAWFUL PLACE OF EMPLOYMENT

ISLE OF DOGS OBEDIENCE TRAINING CENTRE + NEWS KENNEL

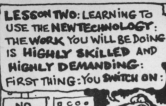

LESSON TWO: LEARNING TO USE THE NEW TECHNOLOGY: THE WORK YOU WILL BE DOING IS HIGHLY SKILLED AND HIGHLY DEMANDING: FIRST THING: YOU SWITCH ON:

NO TALKING

©Steve Bell 1986

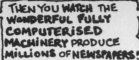

THEN YOU WATCH THE WONDERFUL FULLY COMPUTERISED MACHINERY PRODUCE MILLIONS OF NEWSPAPERS!

NO UNAUTHORISED MOVEMENT

NO TALKING

SHOULD ANYTHING GO WRONG YOU SIMPLY PRESS THE 'OFF' BUTTON AND BLOW YOUR DOG WHISTLE. THE COLOUR-CODED MAINTENANCE SUPERVISOR DOGS WILL THEN APPEAR....

THE COLOUR-CODED-MAINTENANCE-SUPERVISOR DOGS WILL THEN PERFORM FAULT DIAGNOSIS AND TAKE THE APPROPRIATE COURSE OF ACTION:

WORRGHH...THIS F****N' MACHINE'S F****N' BROKEN!!

I'M GONNA SMASH YOUR F****N' EAD IN, YOU F****N' MARXIST SABOTEUR!!

WELL- YOU'VE BEEN SITTING THERE SEVERAL HOURS NOW AND THIS MOMENT IS WHAT IT'S ALL BEEN FOR: THE FINISHED PRODUCT!! HOW DO YOU FEEL ABOUT IT?

F****N' GREAT, BOSS!!

PISS ON THE PEACE POOFS

DEADLY RAY'S

ZORK... BLIT... BLIT...

OFF ON

©Steve Bell 1986

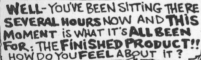

WHAT DO YOU THINK OF IT CONTENT-WISE? DOES IT REFLECT YOUR CONCERNS, YOUR DESIRES AND YOUR NEEDS AS AN ECONOMIC UNIT??

YES BOSS PLEASE BOSS- CAN I GO TO THE TOILET PLEASE, BOSS??

WE SAY- FLOG THE WOG DOG

OFF ON

DON'T YOU AGREE ABOUT THE OVERWHELMING NEED TO END CLASS CONFLICT BY CRUSHING ANY WORKER'S ORGANIS-ATION??

YES BOSS- PLEASE BOSS PISS BOSS PLEASE?

O.K. OFF YOU GO!!

THUMP THE THUGS NOW

ATTENTION! PINK DOG IN BLUE ZONE!

RRING

BIP

HONEST MARGARET'S
BONA·FIDE·OFF·THE·BACK·OF·A·LORRY
BOOT SALE

NEXT ORFF: UNDERWEAR, AND PRICES, THE LIKE OF WHICH YOU WILL NOT HAVE SEEN IN ALL YOUR BORN DAYS!!

PANTS — NOT A PAHND A PAIR, NOT 50p A PAIR, NOT EVEN 25p A PAIR...

© Steve Bell 1986

I'M OFFERIN' YOU FULL SIZED MENS' UNDERPANTS AT 5p A PAIR, AND NOT ONLY THAT—HONEST MARGARETS UNDERPANTS 'AVE A UNIQUE FEATURE:—

...THEY COME READY WARMED FOR YOUR PERSONAL COMFORT!!

'23'

FTWANG

HONEST MARGARET
BONA FIDE·BACK·OF·A·LORRY
BOOT SALE

'232'

RIGHT! NEXT ORFF IS GAS! YOU CAN'T SEE IT, YOU CAN'T TOUCH IT, BUT YOU CAN SMELL IT ALRIGHT!

...AS WITNESS MY CHUNKY FRIEND NIGEL 'ERE — GORN BENNETT!! 'E'S DONE IT AGAIN! 'E'S DROPPED ANOTHER ORSON* WHAT A PEN + INK, LADIES AND GENTS!!

* ORSON KART-FART

BELIEVE ME FOLKS — ONE MILLION CUBIC FEET OF GAS A DAY FROM THIS BOY.... WHAT AM I BID??

CLICK

© Steve Bell 1986

BOOM!

SOLD TO THE BAKED BEAN IN THE COWBOY HAT!

117

© Steve Bell 1986

HONEST MARGARET'S BONA FIDE OFF·THE·BACK·OF·A·LORRY BOOT SALE

NEXT ORFF LADIES AND GENTS — A ONCE IN A LIFETIME OPPORTUNITY!

WE ARE OFFERING A GILT·EDGED COPPER BOTTOMED ONCE AND ONCE ONLY BIG BIG BARGAIN:

1233

LARGE TEAMS OF MY BOYS HAVE BEEN SIPHONING OFF BILLIONS OF GALLONS OF PRIME QUALITY PRODUCT TO BRING TO YOU AT NEVER TO BE REPEATED PRICES!...

THE RIVER THAMES!! THIS IS YOUR CHANCE TO OWN ONE OF BRITAIN'S OLDEST AND LOVELIEST WATERWAYS. HONEST MARGARET ® GUARANTEE DELIVERY ANYWHERE IN THE WORLD!!

THANKS TO HEATHER

HONEST MARGARET'S BONA FIDE OFF·THE·BACK·OF·A·LORRY BOOT SALE

FINALLY LADIES AND GENTS I 'AVE A QUESTION FOR YOU:

© Steve Bell 1986

ARE YOU TIRED OF PEOPLE DOIN' YOU OVER AND NICKIN' YOUR STUFF?? ARE YOU FED UP WITH PEOPLE TELLIN' PORKYPIES IN PUBLIC PLACES??

ARE YOU SICKENED BY THE CONTINUED DECLINE IN MORAL STANDARDS IN THIS ONCE GREAT NATION OF OURS??? I'M ASKIN' YOU TO GET UP ORFF YOUR BUMS AND BUY SOMETHING THAT WILL CHANGE YOUR LIVES...

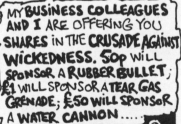

MY BUSINESS COLLEAGUES AND I ARE OFFERING YOU SHARES IN THE CRUSADE AGAINST WICKEDNESS. 50p WILL SPONSOR A RUBBER BULLET; £1 WILL SPONSOR A TEAR GAS GRENADE; £50 WILL SPONSOR A WATER CANNON.....

1234

QUINT HAS GONE INTO LABOUR, THOUGH NOT IN THE POLITICAL SENSE...

YOU'RE IN LUCK, YOUR LORDSHIP-YOUR CONSULTANT MR. McMAMMON IS GOING TO DO YOUR DELIVERY IN PERSON!

NNGH!

1237

NOW I'M JUST GOING TO WIRE YOU UP TO THIS HUGE MACHINE...

©SteveBell 1986

WHAT DOES IT DO? DON'T YOU WORRY YOUR LITTLE HEAD ABOUT THAT...

...JUST YOU TRY AND RELAX!!

MOOP BEEP

CITY CLOSING PRICES

KLANK KLANK

NOW WHAT WOULD YOU LIKE IN THE WAY OF A PAINKILLER?

MEEP

1238

YOU MEAN...IT'S GOING TO HURT??

YEAH! NOT HALF!! YOU CAN HAVE GAS AND AIR...BUT I SUPPOSE YOU'VE ALREADY HAD A SURFEIT OF THAT IN THE HOUSE OF LORDS...

...OR THERE'S PETHADINE, WHICH GETS YOU AND THE BABY NICE N' MELLOW, OR IF YOU REALLY WANT TO GET SERIOUS WE CAN DO AN EPIDURAL...LOTS OF TUBES AND STUFF!

I THINK I'LL HAVE AN EXTRA LARGE PORT, PLEASE

NO! NO! NO!! THIS IS A HOSPITAL WE CAN'T POSSIBLY HAVE YOU INTRODUCING THAT SORT OF THING INTO YOUR SYSTEM!!

©SteveBell '86

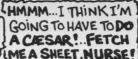

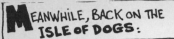

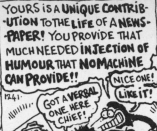

DID YOU KNOW..?

...THAT WORLD FAMOUS NEWS MAGNATE RUPERT MURDOCH HAS ONLY GOT ONE TESTICLE??

1245

...THAT THE BIGGEST TITS IN THE WORLD BELONG TO THE STATUE OF LIBERTY IN NEW YORK, U.S.A??

...THAT IF YOU LAID EVERY SUN READER END TO END THEY WOULD STRETCH FROM WAPPING TO RUPERT MURDOCH'S BIRTHPLACE IN AUSTRALIA??

~ © Steve Bell 1986 ~

...THAT BEING LAID END TO END IS THE CLOSEST THING TO MENTAL STIMULATION MOST SUN READERS ARE EVER LIKELY TO GET??

OLD DOGBREATH'S
PRE & POST HOLOCAUST GARDENING TIPS

2 ft. 6 ins
2 ft 6 ins

~ © Steve Bell 1986 ~

5 ft

1246

NO BROKEN BOTTLES

MEANWHILE IN PECKHAM:

OKAY, THIS IS IT!! ISSUE NUMBER ONE OF "THE CREATURE" IS ABOUT TO BE 'PUT TO BED' ON THE LATEST CAST-OFF RONEO TECHNOLOGY!

© Steve Bell 1986

THE AUTHENTIC VOICE OF INNER LONDON WILDLIFE IS POISED TO HIT THE STREETS!! O.K! SWITCH ON!!

BONK

IT'S LOOKING GOOD!! SWITCH TO FULL POWER!!

CHAKKADA CHAKKADA CHAKKADA

1247

STOP!! STOP!! HOLD THE FRONT PAGE!! CHANGE EVERYTHING!! WE'VE GOT TO FIT IN THIS GREAT NEW PICTURE OF THE QUEEN!!

WE SAY... PISS ON THE MONARCHY

MEANWHILE ON THE **ISLE OF DOGS**:

THIS IS IT — THE FIRST **MAJOR PERK** OF BEING A NEWSPAPER OWNER — A **BIG DINNER IN THE CITY**!!

© Steve Bell 1986

THE WORSHIPFUL COMPANY OF BURGLARS SWINDLERS MONEY JUGGLERS

PSSSSSSST PSSSS PSSS

BIG ROVER, BIG FIDO AND HIS HIGHNESS **PRINCE PENGUIN**!

1248

127

A BIG DINNER IN THE CITY:

LOOK AT ALL THIS **CUTLERY**, BIG ROVER – THIS IS HOW THE **REAL QUALITY** DOWN THEIR **GRUB!** THAT'S A **QUAIL FORK!!**

...AND THAT'S A **NIGEL LAWSON** FORK FOR EFFICIENT PLATE CLEARANCE....

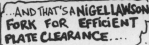

1249.
...AND THAT'S A POST-PRANDIAL NOSEPICKER

MAYLANDS HALAYDEES HENNA GENHOOLMAN

HAY CALL UPON THEHA RAIGHT HONORAYBULL DOCTOR DAI D. DEATH...

IN MY JUDGEMENT FOR MYSELF I WOULD SAY PERSONALLY...

1250

...THAT IN MY EXPERIENCE IN GOVERNMENT, INDEED AS FOREIGN SECRETARY...

I BELIEVE, AND I THINK RIGHTLY SO, THAT NOT ONLY MUST SENSIBLE GOVERNMENT DARE TO CARE....

IT MUST ALSO ACKNOWLEDGE THE OVERWHELMING NEED FOR GREED!!

Y'LITTLE BEAUTY!!

129

IT'S BEEN A **WHOLE WEEK** WITHOUT A LEAK OF **RADIO ACTIVE STEAM**, LARRY — I'VE GOT THE SHAKES REAL **BAAAAA·A·A·A·D!!**

WE'VE GOTTA **DO SOMETHING**, LAZ!!

BNFL
~~WINDSCALE~~
~~SELLAFIELD~~
LEAFY MEADOW
EEZI KLEEN CHEEP
POWER PLANT

1257

...WE'VE GOT TO **BREAK** THE **CYCLE OF ADDICTION!!** WE'VE GOT TO PULL OURSELVES **BACK** FROM **THE BRINK!**

YEAH! YEAH!! HOW?

...WE'VE GOT TO **RE·EDUCATE OURSELVES!!** WE'VE GOT TO REDUCE OUR DEPENDENCY ON APPARENTLY CHEAP BUT **ACTUALLY LETHAL ENERGY SOURCES!!**

WE'VE GOT TO LEARN TO **DO** WITHOUT HAIR·DRYERS, TOASTERS COLOUR T.V.s, CURLING·TONGS, FOOD PROCESSORS, COMPACT DISC PLAYERS....

THAT'S GONNA LEAVE **ONE HELL OF A GAPING HOLE IN MY** LIFESTYLE, LARRY!

© Steve Bell 1986

IT'S **CRIMINAL** WHAT THEY'RE DOING IN THERE, LAZ — THEY SEEM TO WANT TO **FILL THE WORLD** WITH **INDESTRUCTIBLE POISONOUS CRUD**, YET ALL THE TIME THERE'S A **MAJOR BENIGN + WHOLLY UNEXPLOITED** ENERGY SOURCE STARING THEM IN THE FACE...

WHAT'S THAT, LARRY?

1258.

I'M TALKING ABOUT **SHEEPFARTS**, LAZ!!

SHEEPFARTS?

YEAH, SHEEPFARTS — I HEARD SOMEWHERE THAT IF THEY HARNESSED THE POWER OF **ALL THE SHEEPFARTS IN THE WORLD**, THEY'D HAVE ENOUGH ENERGY TO DRIVE A LANDROVER TO **BETELGEUSE!!**

THAT'S **INCREDIBLE**, LARRY — MIND YOU, IF I HAD A LAND· ROVER I WOULDN'T FART ABOUT GOING TO **BETELGEUSE**

I DON'T THINK YOU'VE QUITE GOT THE POINT, LAZ!!

© Steve Bell 1986

AS I WURLK ALURNG THE ♪♫ AVENUE GORDON-BENNETT * WITH URN EENDEPENDENTAIRE...

* IT REALLY EXISTS

1259

...YOU CAN 'EAR THE GAIRLS DECLAIRE..... ♫ ♪

'OO'S THAT WURLY OVAIR THAIRE??

WITH MA EASEL AND MA BURX OF PANTS ♪♫ AND MA LEEDLE FURLDING CHAIR...

© Steve Bell 1986

AH'M THE MAN 'OO PANTS THE DUCKS IN THE PLACE DU TERTRE !! ♫

YOU LARK A LARKNESS DURN?

ÊRGUE!! POUFFE!! AH'M SO PEESTARFE!! I AM JUSTE URN 'ACK!!

1260

AH'M SICK TO DEATH OF STUPIDE RO'OBERE NECKINGUE POOBLEEK! ALL THEY WURNT IS PANTINGS OF BIG EYED BRATS!!

NUR PEECTURES!

...OR MAYBE REVURLTINGUE VIEWS OF THE STINKINGUE PLACE DU TERTRE, NURT TO MENTION 'ORREEBLE DURCKS ON VELVET!! ÊRGUE!! PTUI!!!

I SAY STURFF THIS !!! I AM AN ARTISTE! I SHOULD BE LARK RUBENS – – PANTING 'UGE CANVASSES FULL OF NEKKED WEEMEN FOR ENURMOUS AMOUNTS OF MURNEY!!!

© Steve Bell '86

YOU WANNA FEW DUCKS BOTTOM LEFT? NO PROBLEM!

AH'M GETTING URP! AH FEEL INSPARRED!! TODAY I PANT MAMASTÈRE·PISS!!

NOW AH KNURR THE SICRET OF SOOCCESS!! I'AVE TO PANT NEKKED WEEMEN AND RURLTY!!!

PUMMEL SPLAT!

© Steve Bell 1986

IT'S CALLED: "THE ARRAIVAL OF THE ROYAL COOPLE AT 'ARRODS" THE 'ELICOPTAIRE REPRESENTS THE CAREFREE SPIRIT OF YOUTH; THE KNEELING SOOPLICANT IS THE ARCHBEESHURP OF CARTERBURY; THE GONG PLONQUE SYMBOL-AHSES THE MORRIAGE CEREMONY; THE THREE NEKKED WEEMEN REPRESENT CHASTITY, OBEDIENCE AND MARITAL FIDELITÉ; THE TROMPETING ANGEL REPRESENTS THE BBC....

-1263-

135

ALL OVER AMERICA, FARTBAGS ARE LEVITATING:

THIS IS IT!! IT'S THE RAPTURE!! WE'RE GOIN' UP T'HEAVEN!

WE'RE CROSSING THE LINE OF DEATH, CHIEF!

WHEE!

1264

YOU'RE ON YOUR OWN, LUKE— THE FORCE BE WITH YOU!

© Steve Bell 1986

SCORE 58 AYRAB FANATICS SCORE 116 AYRAB FANATICS SCORE 143 AYRAB FANATICS AND RISING....

PEEYOOW PEEYOOW PEEPEEPEE PEEYOOW

POOP!

POP!

WHAT'S HAPPENIN'?

WHERE AM I? WHAT'S THAT TERRIBLE SMELL??

KRUMP

DEMOCRACY IN ACTION ON CAPITOL HILL:

I'VE GOT NO TAHM TO TALK WITH THE MEEJA NOW, BOY!

SENATOR VENAL BUNNY-SHOOT— HOW WILL YOU BE VOTING TODAY, SIR?

SENATOR, THE ZBC NEWS NETWORK HOPES THAT YOU WILL ACCEPT THIS DONATION TO THE HELP THE HUNGRY REELECT BUNNY'SHOOT TRUST!

WHY THANKYOU, BOY!

AH'M GOING TO BE VOTIN' TO INCREASE HUMAN MILITARIAN AID TO THE FREEDOM FIGHTERS IN HONDURAS AND THE SIXTH FLEET... NOW IF YOU'LL EXCUSE ME....

© Steve Bell 86

...I HAVE TO MEET WITH A LOBBY DELEGATION OF IMPORTANT HIGH RANKING VIDEO GAMES!!!

GOOK INCURSION

STAR WARS

-1265-

ON CAPITOL HILL:

SENATOR BUCK METHANE — HOW DO YOU RESPOND TO REPORTS THAT...

...THE INVASION OF NICARAGUAN TROOPS INTO HONDURAS OCCURRED ONLY IN THE IMAGINATION OF U.S. EMBASSY STAFF IN TEGUCIGALPA??

IT SURPRISES ME YOU SHOULD ASK THAT...

1266

I DON'T WISH TO ENGAGE IN PHILOSOPHICAL SPECULATION WITH YOU AT THIS MOMENT IN TIME, BUT THE FACT REMAINS THAT, WHETHER REAL OR IMAGINARY...

...THE **THREAT TO U.S. INTERESTS** POSED BY SUCH AN **INVASION** IS **EXTREMELY DISTURBING** TO ALL THOSE WHO CARE ABOUT **FREEDOM**. I BELIEVE THE FREEDOM TO FANTASISE SUCH INCURSIONS IS ONE THAT SHOULD BE PROTECTED **AT ALL COSTS!**

THIS LATEST **SO-CALLED SOVIET OFFER** IS NOTHING BUT A **CHEAP PROPAGANDA PLOY**....

...THIS IS **T.V. DIPLOMACY** AT IT'S MOST **SQUALID,** AIMING TO **SOW CONFUSION** IN THE MINDS.....

AIMING TO SOW CONFUSION IN THE MINDS OF GULSKI

1267

...OF **GULLIBLE ELEMENTS** WITHIN CIVIL POPULATIONS OF THE **WESTERN ALLIANCE** AND MISLEAD THEM AS TO TRUE SOVIET INTENTIONS.

HOLY BOWELS OF GOD!! MY **HAIR** JUST **CROSSED THE LINE OF DEATH!** SHOOT IT DOWN! SHOOT IT DOWN!!

CUT!! CUT!! WE'D BETTER GO FOR A RETAKE HERE, MR. PRESIDENT!!

A CONCERNED MONKEY LOOKS OUT OVER THE CAPITAL:

WHO RUNS THIS CITY SINCE THE DEMISE OF THE GLC, KIPLING?

A LOAD OF QUANGOS, JOHN

© Steve Bell 1986

WHAT IS A QUANGO EXACTLY, KIPLING?

A QUANGO IS A QUASI-AUTONOMOUS NON-GOVERNMENTAL ORGANISATION

THEY'RE BASICALLY A LOAD OF UNELECTED BUREAUCRATS

BUT WHAT ARE THEY, AND WHAT DO THEY DO?

LOOK - HERE'S AN EXAMPLE - AN AD IN THE LOCAL RAG - "HAVING POLLUTION OR ENVIRONMENTAL PROBLEMS IN THE OLD GLC AREA?"

".. YOU SHOULD HENCEFORTH REFER TO THE DISTRICT AUDITORS LONDON ENVIRONMENT KOMMITTEE .... KOMMITTEE WITH A 'K' — I WONDER WHY THAT SHOULD BE?

1270

DALEKS HAVE TAKEN OVER RESPONSIBILITY FOR LOCAL GOV'T IN THE GREATER LONDON AREA....

WE ARE RES·PONS·IBLE DA·LEKS...

1271

INSIDE COUNTY HALL:

WE ARE DEMO·CRAT·IC DA·LEKS THE MO·TION IS "WE WILL EX·TERMINATE!"

ALL THOSE IN·FAVOUR RAISE THEIR RIGHT PLUN·GER

ALL THOSE A·GAINST RAISE THEIR LEFT PLUNGER

BUT DALEKS DON'T HAVE LEFT PLUN·GERS DA·LEKS ON·LY HAVE LEFT EXTERMINATORS!

© Steve Bell 1986

EX·ACT·LY·WE WILL·EXTERMIN·ATE·CARRIED UNAN·IMOUSLY!!!

141

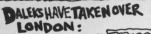

DALEKS HAVE TAKEN OVER LONDON:

ITEM ONE: THE RISING TIDE OF **BLACK LESBIAN TROTSKYIST PERMISSIVE EXTREMISM**....

EXTERMINATE EXTERMINATE

ITEM TWO: CYCLING LANES AND FREE BUS AND TUBE PASSES IN GREATER LONDON...

1272

EXTERMINATE EXTERMINATE

ITEM THREE: UN ACCOUNT ABLE SLUMP IN DALEK POPULARITY WHY??

WE HAVE THE POLICY ABOUT RIGHT THE PROBLEM IS ONE OF PRESENTATION.

© Steve Bell 1986

WHAT IS TO BE DONE?

EXTERMINATE USING PLUNGERS ONLY!!

WHAT'S THE MATTER WITH ME DOCTOR? I CAN'T SEEM TO CONCENTRATE ON ANYTHING PEOPLE LAUGH AT ME ON THE STREET.....

I MAY BE HAVING A MID LIFE CRISIS I THINK I MAY BE IMPOTENT.

1273

I NO LONGER STRIKE TERROR IN THE HEARTS OF THE PUNTERS.... ONLY THE OTHER DAY AN OLD LADY ASKED ME TO UN BLOCK HER SINK... I ASK YOU....

VOT VAS YOUR RESPONSE?

I EXTERMINATED HER LINO.....

© Steve Bell 1986

Panel 1: THESE·LEAFY·SUBURBS· ARE·BEDROCK·AREAS·OF· DALEK·SUPPORT·

© Steve Bell 1986

Panel 2: SIR·CAN·WE·COUNT· ON·YOUR·VOTE·IN·THE· FORTH·COMING·BOROUGH· ELECTIONS??····

NO, MATE — I'M JUST THE CHAUFFEUR.

Panel 3: I SAY, DAMMIT — —WHAT DO YOU THINK YOU'RE DOING THERE??

Panel 4: SIR·CAN·WE·COUNT·ON· YOUR·SUPPORT·FOR·OUR· POLICY·OF·KEEP·ING·DOWN· THE·RATES·AND·THE·LOWER· CLASS·ES?? ABSOLUTELAH! I'VE VOTED DALEK ALL MY LIFE AND I'M NOT ABOUT TO CHANGE!!!! NOW SWEEP UP THAT PILE OF ASH AND GET ORFF M'LAWN, Y'LITTLE TIN MONSTAH!!

274

Panel 5: PHASE·TWO·OF·DALEK· POP·U·LAR·ITY·CAMPAIGN· ·SEEK·OUT·AND·IDENTIFY· SLOANE·RANGER·SUPPORT·

1275·

Panel 6: WE·MUST·CON·VINCE· THEM·THAT·WE·HAVE·THEIR· INTERESTS·AT·HEART·····

A.K. YAH! A.K. YAH!

© Steve Bell 1986

Panel 7: A.K.YAH! HIGH DELIGHTFUL! DA·LEKS·OBEY· HEREDITARY· WEALTH·WITHOUT· ·QUESTION···

Panel 8: YAH! COULD YOU DO SOMETHING ABITE BUILDING A RANGE RAVER LANE THROUGH THAT CYNECIL HIGHZING ESTATE OVER THERE? AKYAH AKYAH ·YOUR·WISH ·IS·OUR· COMMAND!

143

THE OTHER THING I CAN'T STOMACH IS THE **TORRENT OF BILGE AND LIES** POURING OUT OF **BBC RADIO** — **MIDDLE-CLASS** AND POINTS RIGHT — WARDS. **HOW DUTIFULLY** THEY VOMIT OUT WHATEVER THE GOV- — ERNMENT CARES TO FEED THEM : "THE F. ONE ELEVENS ARE ON A ROUTINE EXERCISE... OOH! GOOD- NESS ME!! THEY SEEM TO HAVE **BOMBED LIBYA !!!**"

"WE ARE **ASSURED** THERE IS **PROOF** THAT **GADDAFY MURDERED BAMBI'S MUM,** BUT WE CAN'T RELEASE IT FOR **REASONS OF NATIONAL SECURITY !!** " HAH! KEEP THEM **IGNORANT** KEEP THEM **STUPID!** FEED THEM A **FEW** MORE SELECT **PORK PIES !!!**

BUT YOU'RE SURELY NOT EXPECTING A MORE OPEN SOCIETY IN LENINGRAD ??

FROM WHAT **I** SEE THE AVER- AGE SOVIET **PUNTER** HAS A **DAMN SIGHT SANER VIEW** OF WHAT'S GOING ON IN THE WORLD THAN YOU'RE EVER LIKELY TO GET FROM **BBC APOLOGISTS** FOR **IMPERIALIST MADNESS !!**

BUT WHAT ABOUT ALL THE **DISSIDENTS ?**

© Steve Bell 1986

WHAT ABOUT **EL SALVADOR ?!** WHERE WOULD **YOU** PREFER TO BE A **DISSIDENT? POLAND** WHERE YOU MIGHT GET A **JAIL TERM,** OR **EL SALVADOR** WHERE YOU MIGHT GET A NICE "**DEMOCRATIC" DEATH SQUAD ??** AND THAT **BASTARD REAGAN** HAS THE **NERVE** TO **PONTIFICATE** ABOUT **TERROR !!**

SKULLPTT

KIPLING IS **HOLDING FORTH** ABOUT HIS **IMMINENT DEFECTION:**

AS FAR AS **I** CAN SEE, REAGAN'S FOREIGN POLICY HAS ALL THE **HALLMARKS OF SIXTIES SPOILT BRAT-ISM** WITH NONE OF ITS **REDEEMING FEATURES** — AT LEAST THEY WERE AGAINST A **WAR** — THIS MANIAC IS SET ON **STARTING THEM** ALL OVER THE PLACE !!!

EVERYTHING THE U.S. GOV'T DOES IS CALCULATED TO **MANIPULATE** AN **ILL- INFORMED** AND **ILL- REPRESENTED** "PUBLIC OPINION". THE NEEDS OF **EVERYONE ELSE** ON EARTH ARE SUBORDINATE TO THE PLEASURING OF THAT **IGNORANT OVERSTUFFED ENTITY !!**

I THINK IT'S HIGHTIME WE STOOD UP FOR OUR- SELVES AGAINST DESE LIBYAN BUMS

THEN THAT **BASTARD** HAS THE **CHEEK** TO TURN ROUND AND CALL THE SOVIET PROPOSALS ON DISARMAMENT '**A PROPAGANDA PLOY**"!! **CHRIST!!** EVERYTHING THAT NO-LONGER-VERY-FUNNY-CLOWN DOES IS DONE WITH THE **SOLE AIM** OF **PEDDLING PROPAGANDA**

1281

© Steve Bell 1986

OK, WELL, I'VE HAD ENOUGH !! CALL ME A **DUPE** OR A **STOOGE** IF YOU LIKE, BUT I'M DEFECTING TO LENINGRAD **TOOT SWEET !!**

YOU'RE JUST MISSING YOUR FRIEND **GARONYA,** AREN'T YOU ??

THERE MAY BE A **SLIGHT ELEMENT** OF THAT.... THE TROUBLE IS — I HAVEN'T GOT THE **FARE MONEY.** DO YOU THINK THERE'S ANY CHANCE OF GETTING A **SPECIAL NEEDS GRANT** FROM THE **DHSS ??**

THE AUTHOR MAKES NO APOLOGY FOR THE LACK OF JOKES THIS WEEK.

146

SNAT
SNAT!

DON'T KNOW MUCH ABOUT **HISTORY**... DON'T CARE MUCH ABOUT **SOCI·ETY**...♪

DON'T CARE MUCH ABOUT **READIN' BOOKS**... DON'T CARE MUCH ABOUT **STARVIN' GOOKS**....
© Steve Bell 1986

BUT I KNOW THAT IF **I BOMB YOU** AND IF YOU TRY TO **BOMB ME TOO**... ♪

...**WHAT A WONDERFUL WAR** IT WOULD BE !!♪

APOLOGIES TO SAM COOKE.

1282.

NOTHING IS SAFE ANY MORE IN AN **UNSTABLE WORLD** :

AAAAAAARRRGGH!! SHOT THROUGH THE **HEAD** BY A **LIBYAN IRANIAN SUICIDE MIDGET** CONCEALED IN MY **CHEESEBURGER!**

WHEW! GOOD JOB THEY GOT ME THERE, OTHERWISE I'D BE A **DEAD MAN !!** ...BUT **WAIT**... I'VE HAD A SUDDEN **BLINDING FLASH OF INTELLIGENCE** THROUGH THIS **HOLE** IN MY HEAD!!
© Steve Bell 1986

I KNOW NOW THAT **GADAFY** IS JUST A **PUNK**. THE **WORLD LEADER IN TERRORIST SPONSORSHIP** IS **NOT** HE, NO SIR!!!

IT IS **I**, RONALD WILSON **MAD DOG REAGAN**, AND I'M GOING TO HAVE TO **TEACH MYSELF A LESSON I WON'T HURRIEDLY FORGET !!!**

1283

147

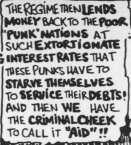

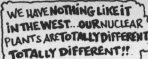

YOU KNOW THIS IS A VERY VERY VERY VERY SERIOUS ACCIDENT INDEED IN THE UKRAINE...

CAREFUL WHAT YOU'RE SAYING..

THERE MAY BE THOUSANDS DEAD AND DYING, WHICH OF COURSE RAISES QUESTIONS...

..ABOUT THE ENTIRE FUTURE OF NUCLEAR POWER.

NO, NO, LET'S NOT JUMP TO RASH CONCLUSIONS. IT RAISES QUESTIONS ABOUT THE ENTIRE FUTURE OF THE SOVIET NUCLEAR INDUSTRY, WHICH OF COURSE BEARS ABSO- -LUTELY NO RELATION TO THE NUCLEAR INDUSTRY IN THE WEST WHERE, BECAUSE OF STRINGENT SAFETY PROCEDURES, DRIFTING CLOUDS OF RADIO- ACTIVE DEATH ARE JUST NOT ON, FRANKLY

1292.

IT ALSO PROVIDES A FINE OPPORTUNITY FOR IDEOLOGICAL POINT SCORING IN THE CONTINUING GLOBAL STRUGGLE BETWEEN THE EVIL EMPIRE AND THE WINDS OF FREEDOM, OR DOES IT?? ONLY TIME WILL TELL. THIS IS LARRY THE TWO HEADED SHEEP, NEWS AT TEN, LEAFY MEADOW.

WHERE AM I?

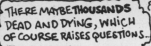

LET'S FACE IT, IT COULDN'T HAPPEN HERE BECAUSE WE'VE GOT THE BEST AND SAFEST NUCLEAR INDUSTRY IN THE WORLD

GIMME AN 'S'! S!

© Steve Bell 1986

WE'VE GOT THE BEST AND FREEST PRESS IN THE WORLD, THE BEST TELEVISION IN THE WORLD, THE BEST SYSTEM OF DEMOCRACY, THE FINEST JUDICIAL SYSTEM MONEY CAN BUY

GIMME AN 'H'! H!

THE BEST HEALTH SERVICE, THE BEST PUBLIC LIBRARIES THE BEST EDUCATION SYSTEM

GIMME AN "EEP"! EEP!!

1293.

THE BEST AGRICULTURAL INDUSTRY, THE BEST ROYAL FAMILY, THE BEST FOOTBALL TEAM, THE BEST PRISON SYSTEM, THE BEST NUCLEAR WASTE DISPOSAL SYSTEM...

BURY + FORGE LTD

WHASSAT SPELL? SHEEP! WHASSAT SPELL? SHEEP!

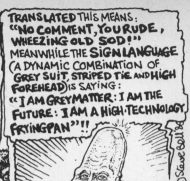

SPOKE YOURSELF PUNDIT

1296.

NEXT WE HAVE DEFENSIVE PUNDITRY AS DEPLOYED AGAINST PATHOLOGICALLY HOSTILE INTERVIEWING TECHNIQUES:

THIS IS A RICH COMBINATION OF MIDDLE ENGLISH, HIGH PUNDIT AND COMPLEX SIGN LANGUAGE. HERE WE HAVE A TYPICAL EXCHANGE.

WELL, MR SO-CALLED ACCEPTABLE PINKO— THE ELECTORS OF LIVERPOOL CERTAINLY SEEM TO HAVE COCKED A SNOOK AT YOUR ANTI-MILITANT PURGE. CAN YOU SERIOUSLY SIT THERE AND TELL ME YOUR PARTY IS ANY LONGER A CREDIBLE PARTY OF GOVERNMENT?

WITH RESPECT SIR ROBIN WE'RE DELIGHTED THAT THE LABOUR PARTY HAS RETAINED CONTROL OF LIVERPOOL.

TRANSLATED THIS MEANS: "NO COMMENT, YOU RUDE, WHEEZING OLD SOD!" MEANWHILE THE SIGN LANGUAGE (A DYNAMIC COMBINATION OF GREY SUIT, STRIPED TIE AND HIGH FOREHEAD) IS SAYING: "I AM GREY MATTER: I AM THE FUTURE: I AM A HIGH-TECHNOLOGY FRYING PAN"!!

SPOKE YOURSELF PUNDIT

1297.

NOW WE HAVE THE HEAVY-DUTY COMMENTATORS: THIS IS REALLY SERIOUS A-LEVEL PUNDITRY:

WELL, THERE'S BEEN A SWING, A GOOD SWING, BUT IS IT A SIGNIFICANT SWING TO THE LABOUR PARTY? A VERY GOOD SWING FOR THE ALLIANCE, BUT IS IT VERY GOOD ENOUGH?

THERE'S NO DOUBT THAT IT'S BEEN A DEVASTATING NIGHT FOR THE CONSERVATIVES, BUT HAS IT BEEN AS DEVASTATING AS IT COULD HAVE BEEN? I THINK THE FIGURES BEAR ME OUT WHEN I ANSWER "NO" TO ALL THESE QUESTIONS.

TRANSLATED, THIS MEANS: "WHEN I CHOPPED UP MY CHICKEN THIS MORNING IT SHAT ALL OVER ME. THIS IS WIDELY AGREED TO BE A FAVOURABLE OMEN. THUS I FORESEE GREAT PROSPECTS FOR PURVEYORS OF INCON-SEQUENTIAL CLAPTRAP LIKE ME."

IN BROAD STATISTICAL TERMS I'D AGREE WITH THAT.

AND NOW, THE MOMENT YOU'VE BEEN WAITING FOR: THE MOMENT YOU CAN TRY OUT YOUR NEWLY LEARNED PUNDITRY IN THE "SPOKE YOURSELF PUNDIT" CONVERSATION CLASS! HERE ARE THE OTHER MEMBERS:

SPEAKING FOR THE CONSERVATIVES GENGHINA KHAZI M.P.:

ON BEHALF OF THE SDP: DICK HEAD Q.C.

...AND TONIGHT'S TOKEN LEFT-WING ELEMENT, GENERAL SECRETARY OF THE DOGGY DYNAMO'S UNION: ERIC ORGAN.

WHAT DO YOU MEAN YOU DON'T WANT TO SPEAK TO ANY OF THESE PEOPLE??

© Steve Bell '86

I'LL KICK OFF TONIGHT'S "SPOKE YOURSELF PUNDIT" CONVERSATION CLASS WITH THIS LITTLE NUGGET FROM A MR. BERNARD BOLLOCKS OF BRAINTREE. HE ASKS: "WOULD THE PANEL AGREE THAT WE DON'T ACTUALLY HAVE A THREE-PARTY SYSTEM AS SUCH, RATHER WE HAVE TWO TWO-PARTY SYSTEMS?" WELL TEAM, WHAT DO YOU THINK??

DICK HEAD Q.C.??

OH ABSOLUTELY! I THINK MR. FINGER HAS PUT HIS BOLLOCKS ON IT: PART OF THE COUNTRY IS ALLIANCE-V-TORIES; THE OTHER PART IS ALLIANCE-V-LABOUR. VERY MUCH SO!!

© Steve Bell 1986

GENGHINA KHAZI??

I'M AFRAID I'M GOING TO HAVE TO CORRECT YOU, DICK, BUT YOU WON'T OBJECT BECAUSE OF MY YOUTH AND CHARM - YOU SEE, PART OF THE COUNTRY IS TORIES-V-ALLIANCE, BUT THE OTHER PART IS TORIES-V-LABOUR!

WELL WE COULD GO ON ALL NIGHT WITH THIS SORT OF GRIPPING STUFF......

AAAAAAAAAARRGHH!

- POP!

WHERE AM I?

MONKEY SLAYS 'JAP T.V. SET' IN HIS SLEEP HORROR